The One That Got Away

The Kind of Love
You Never Recover From

LEE ROBERT SCHREIBER

VOLT PRESS
Los Angeles

"You Never Miss Your Water"
Written by Lightning Hopkins
Used by permission of Prestige Music/Concord Music Group, Inc.

"Devil Got My Woman"
Written by Nehemiah Skip James
Used by permission of Wynwood Music Co., Inc.

Library of Congress Cataloging-in-Publication Data

Schreiber, Lee Robert.
   The one that got away : the kind of love you never recover from / Lee Robert Schreiber.
       p. cm.
     ISBN 1-56625-243-1
     1. Schreiber, Lee Robert—Relations with women. 2. Man-woman relationships. 3. Separation (Psychology) I. Title.
HQ801.S4393 2005
306.73—dc22

                                                    2005011841

Volt Press
a division of Bonus Books
1223 Wilshire Blvd., #597
Santa Monica, CA   90403
www.volt-press.com

This one is for my late father,
Julian Schreiber,
who was *always* on time

Acknowledgments

For their contributions to this work, I'm much obliged to Stephanie Adams, Neil Amdur, Bruce Batkin, David Bell, Beth Bernstein, Caralyn Bialo, Steve Blaustein, Vivian Bradbury, Kyung Cho, Jeff Diamond, Phyllis Director, Liz Dolan, Harvey Dorfman, Mary Duffy, Ellen Feinblum, Beth Filler, Devon Freeny, Joanne Friedman, Michael Fischler, David Granger, John Hanc, Dennis Hanowitz, Richard Hire, Neal Hirschfeld, Howie Hochberg, Stan Kleckner, Ted Klein, Ian Kleinert, Sherry Kramer, Mary Ann Kurtz, Paul Lenok, Mon Levinson, Eric Messenger, Scott Miller, Dennis Minogue, Laura Fieber Minogue, Jack Newman, Ben Olan, Jonathan Olsberg, Dan Paisner, Billy Paul, Janet Parker, Stephanie Penate, Andy Price, Arthur Robinson, Carl Rothman, Keith Schreiber, Marion Schreiber, Meryl Schreiber, Ron Sheppard, John Silbersack, Jeff Stern, Steve Strauss, Paula Weissman, Rick Wolff, and Harv Zimmel, as well as to a wide, warm, and deep circle of friends and family too numerous to mention. Thank you all.

Prologue

Always Something There to Remind Me

It may be the same for women, but here I type first-hand: Men are a sentimental lot. We readily attach ourselves to the past. We resist letting go. And, when forced to move on, we *ache* just like little boys.

> **PHIL,** 54, 6′1″, 205 lbs.; brown eyes; throws right; bespectacled; thinning curly gray hair; literary agent; married on his 51st birthday, almost 40 years to the day after his father's fatal heart attack. The night before that tragedy, at age 11, Phil threw a tantrum, yelling at his father and storming off to bed. They never spoke again. After many, many years of therapy, and the love of an understanding woman, he now acknowledges that maybe his dad's death wasn't his fault.

Every hundred days or so, me and the Boys—ranging across the board in age (late twenties to early sixties), class strata, marital and mental health status, racial, political, religious, and sexual orientation, and even gender (some Boys will be girls)—convene at a downtown tavern in a major English-speaking metropolis to ingest meat (or fish) and booze, while digesting a similarly limited, if inexhaustible, supply of topics.

The conversation is always profane, often hilarious, sometimes angry and occasionally regretful. Here's the breakdown by subject:

- Money (5 percent).
- Work (10 percent).
- Sports and Hobbies (12 percent).
- Relationships (12.5 percent).
- Sex (20 percent).

The remaining chunk of intercourse on a typical Boys' Night Out is apportioned to nostalgia ("a wistful or excessively sentimental yearning for return to or of some past period or irrecoverable condition," as per *Merriam-Webster's Collegiate Dictionary, Tenth Edition*). The overarching subject, then, that gives us, by far, greatest pause and consideration is:

- Time (40.5 percent).

In the life and times of every man and (I'm guessing) most women, there is something or someone—a defining moment, a recurring theme, an influential figure, a deceased or lost loved one—that is thought about, pined for, and, on occasion, wept over . . . above all others.

> **CHUNG,** 29, 5'7", 140 lbs.; brown hair and eyes; lefty; unmarried book editor; literally came to blows with his father when Kim, then 56, left his wife and family to be with a woman he'd known as a teenager in Korea but was forbidden to marry because of her low ancestral station.

Boys' Night Out, or the sentiments expressed therein, is not exclusively a male thing.

> **BETH,** 43, 5′4″, 108 lbs.; auburn hair with a gray streak; blue eyes; lefty; never-married jewelry designer/fashion consultant/writer-editor; dated Scott in high school but soon broke up with him because she found him "too comfortable and, well, nice." They became friends. At age 21, they vowed to "marry at 30 if we're both single." At 29, Scott met and married Elyse. Divorced after 12 years of marriage, Scott started dating again, and Beth began to think that "possibly the guy who had been there through everything might be the one." After a brief sexual affair, Scott told Beth that he did not "want to risk losing my best friend." Scott and Beth, both single, remain the best of friends.

Nearly every adult learns to live peaceably with these sweetly bitter recollections, rarely permitting them to become more than a passing upset. However, for a precious, preoccupied few, this *thing* or *one* becomes the single greatest impediment to a life inhabited most fully.

> **LEE;** (let's say deep into his forties and still single, 5′10.5″, 165 lbs.; blue eyes, brown hair, and pale skin) has carried this thing—this torch, this albatross, this cross—for nearly his entire adult life. It has affected him in a multitude of emotionally crippling, unconsciously-subconscious ways. And like a lot of late boomers with arrested development, he's been ambivalent about blooming, late or ever. Lee claims to crave a deep, reciprocal relationship with a woman, but seems stuck on an idealized image of a girl who fractured his 19-year-old heart and then reset and rebroke it a few more times before deciding that she was

ready to marry him. He could not commit to her, so she soon became—and has remained for nearly 25 years—somebody else's wife and the mother of somebody else's children. The only way Lee believes he can finally get free from his past is to confront it. After all this time, he wants to know: "How *does* one inhabit life most fully?"

This is his (my) story.

• • •

Throughout the book, some names and identifying details have been changed by request. On occasion, literary license (arguably, in the service of humor) may stretch a situation beyond its literal occurrence. Separate discussions with friends and acquaintances have been collated and inserted into selected Boys' Night Out situations. In the greater interest of narrative space or pace, a few quotations have been shortened or sharpened; grammar and spelling have also been corrected. Every other essential detail, for all intents and purposes, is unassailably accurate.

1

*It's About Time**

Poor, Poor Pitiful Me

It is the end of the world as I've known it.

"We're going to make a change at second base," says the manager of my Sunday softball team. For four years, I have been the keystone component on a perennial contender in a fast-pitch bar league. I am also the oldest player; and, as such, speculative chatter regarding my play has become increasingly insistent:

- he has trouble in the field seeing the ball off the bat;
- every grounder is an adventure;
- the most he can do at the plate is punch singles into right.

"It's time," the manager says, "for you to accept a greatly reduced role."

I say I'll think about it.

• • •

*To help evoke a mood, a thought, or a time, the book's title, subtitle, chapter heads, and subheads all double as actual song titles. (For identification of the songwriters, please see www.LeeRobertSchreiber.com.)

MANY, MANY YEARS BEFORE . . .

Think Too Much

"We're gonna make a change," Coach White said to me after the first game of the high school freshman baseball season, in which I'd made four errors at shortstop and struck out three times.

Oh, boy. How many times have you heard that phrase? *We're gonna make a change.* That's what they say before they fire you, break up with you, or tell you that your athletic career is over. (Well, that's what they *would be* saying to me when I got older.)

"I'm moving you from short to third," he said. That didn't sound *so* bad. But I'd always been a shortstop; I didn't know how to play any other position. "You think too much," Coach White said. "Every grounder hit to you gets a whole computer analysis: condition of grass *subtracted by* the number of rocks or pebbles likely to affect the ball's bounce *divided by* pitcher's velocity *plus* wind direction *multiplied by* the number of outs, runners on base and Cheerios in your cereal bowl that morning. . . . You're driving yourself—and me—batty."

Coach, you just want me to catch the ball and throw the runner out?

"Yeah," he said. "At third base, you have only an instant to make the play. No time to think, just react."

I could live with that. And I did, until "night blindness" (on dark, cloudy late afternoons, I'd *hear* the ball whiz by my head) effected another position change—to second base—which was surprisingly gritty and challenging. And, after I made that adjustment, it was only a matter of time until the last step down . . . to the bench, as a utility man and occasional pinch hitter.

The End of the Line

I call my softball coach: I quit. I know I still have a few good years in me, but not if, at the start of every season, I have to justify my value to the team, and to my position.

I recently left a weekly basketball game due to bad knees (and a worse temper); with tennis, it was my elbow; and, as for football, it took me well into the new year to recover from our annual Thanksgiving game. The spirit may be willing as ever, but the flesh, bone, and tendons are not.

So that is that. My competitive athletic career is officially over.

Amateur or pro, it's a defining moment in an athlete's life. You're now a *former* athlete.

"Get over it," says my girlfriend, Grace, who believes a man of a certain age (let's say well into his forties) should give up childish pursuits, accept adult responsibilities, and perhaps think about a lasting relationship with a grown-up woman (like, say, her).

> **GRACE**, 43, 5'7.5", 127 lbs.; blond (highlighted) hair; blue eyes; left-handed; sales rep; called off her wedding three days in advance after discovering her fiancé had been stealing money from her. She has never married, probably dated hundreds of men, and has referred to two or three of them as "the loves of my life." I am not one of them.

Grace just doesn't get it (me). This retirement thing isn't some walk in the park. It is a jolt to the core, and not something that I will easily get over.

Ever since I could run, I have spent much of my life competing (a little too intensely, some would say) on playgrounds and courts, in parks and gyms. Besides, softball has a special hold; it is, after all, a form of *baseball*, the pastime rife with dreamy fields of evocative father-son memories, timeless metaphors, mythic meditations on youth and promise . . .

The Beauty of the Days Gone By

Senior year of college, intramural softball championship. I was playing third base, where the catbird's view from this lush green valley was so spectacularly distracting—mountains shimmering on an early evening in late May—that I'd previously bobbled an easy grounder leading to, for the time being, the winning run.

The girl in my life—the *one*—was sitting cross-legged on the first base side, intently watching and rooting for the Meatball Heroes (and her special hero) to come back from a 6–5 deficit to the Delphic fraternity squad that had dominated play for the past three seasons. Within a month, I will graduate and turn 22, and then my sweetie will take another trip to Israel, where she will become engaged to a construction worker, breaking my heart for the third or fourth instance, depending on how strictly you keep score. But, crouched low a few feet off the bag to guard against extra bases, I was suffused with nothing but love—for my girl, nature's beauty, and, of course, the game.

Their cleanup hitter got out in front of a change-up and tagged it pure on the fat part of the wood (metal bats had not yet been perfected) and sent it screaming down the line—my line—where I was already launched airborne, suspended parallel to the ground, my glove hand turning and stretched, reaching beyond my grasp . . .

Phoomph! The sweet onomatopoeia of ball meeting ancient leather, which strained to retain its objective while I tumbled over third base to earth. Inning over. We came back, of course, to win in our bottom half. Redemption regained. Justice triumphant. Love and glory ascendant.

I wondered if victory would ever feel as good again. Adult life beckoned beyond those mountains, and I'd given barely an hour's thought to what sort of life's work I might pursue. But this was not the moment to temper joy with reality; there'd be plenty of opportunities for that. So, savoring every last instant of this scene, my true love and I walked off into the flickering sunset.

Can't Let Go

"Why can't you let it go?" asks Grace (*it* being the ineffable, inescapable memory of a gone-by era, place, and love).

I've been on the business end of this rhetorical question dozens of times, usually when some smart, attractive, relatively sane woman has reached her exasperation point.

"What is it that you miss the most," she continues in a less confrontational, but much more weighted interrogatory, "the girl, the catch, or your youth?"

This is a new one, and a good one. But, in lieu of a reasoned response at the ready, I grab her ass.

"Why are you such an immature jerk," says Grace, echoing most of the other exasperees with whom I've been romantically involved over the past twenty-odd years. "What *is* your problem?" she asks, as if the sum and substance of deeply imbedded neuroses could be so readily encapsulated and corrected.

Grace cites my preoccupation with youth and my idealized memory of that college girlfriend as the likeliest reasons that a real, lasting bond cannot be formed with a flesh-blood-and-estrogen-filled, gravitationally affected, fortyish woman (like, say, *her*).

I am beginning to think she may have a point. This realization, however, comes too late to save us.

"I don't think this is working out," she says (which is just another version of *We're going to make a change*).

It is, we both agree, a change for the best. But it is painful nonetheless. And though we give it the old college try once or twice more—replicating the makeup-breakup template forged by my first love and me once upon a time—we are soon history.

After every breakup (and there have been *many*), I've had to endure the same lame consolation clauses from well-meaning friends and relations. Such as:

- There Are Plenty of Fish in the Sea.
- There's More Than One Way to Skin a Cat.
- You Must Get Right Back on the Horse.

Each anthropomorphic cliché contains the same nugget of conventional wisdom: There is not one "the one."

Philosophically I believe that to be true. But what if they're wrong?

What if you're allotted only one true love a life?

What if, by definition, a soul mate is an irrevocable and absolute post?

And what if you met and left her—or she left you—a long, long, long (well, not *that* long) ago?

It sounds more than a little pathetic, no?

Romantic, though, too.

It is *both* a pathetic and a romantic sight watching a middle-aged man search for his soul mate, refusing to settle for anything—or anyone—less than his heart's desire, rejecting any love that is not truly, madly, deeply.

All Things Must Pass

They say tragedies come in threes (or is that just celebrity deaths?). I am not in any way equating the end of my softball career or the dissolution of a romantic bond with real catastrophe. I am just trying to put into context the petty reality of what we often define as a life crisis.

You dread hearing it your whole life. And then, on a beautiful autumn day, it comes via telephone: "Your father is dead."

An embolism in his left lung burst, instantly killing "dear ol' da" (as he called himself whenever he left a message on my answering machine) three weeks before his 78th birthday. If statistical averages are a valid gauge, this is precisely his time.

Like most men unaccustomed to and unprepared for the gut-racking emotions that grief renders, I become a virtual Tourette-fest of gurgles, snorts, and strangled honks—a steady stream of lamentations never before heard, at least by my ears, coming out of this mouth. Nor is the heretofore-unseen gut-wrenched me a pretty sight: all those years of carefully constructed cool reduced to an ashen ruin. And yet, I do not give a good squawking goddamn that my tough-guy persona—which

I've built from scratch as a shattered, cuckolded 19 year old—is puddling in a bathetic, leaking mess.

I am oblivious to the projection or protection of any man's image except the one whose icy, gray forehead I kiss for the last time.

It's no great secret that fear prevents many humans—especially the males—from confronting their so-called feelings. What are we so afraid of?

I'm guessing that, in addition to worrying that we'll never be able to staunch the flood of emotions once the bulwarks burst, our greatest fears include:

- appearing weak;

- appearing foolish.

And yet, is there a man among us who has never displayed these human sides to another human? If so, who are *you* fooling?

I respond to this emotional upheaval as well as can be expected. Which is a surprise in itself. I may leak and honk aplenty; but I do not, for a change, hang on for dear life. I am able to grieve for my inevitable loss, but also begin to accept it for what it is: my father's exact-timely exit. He went out a little bent but not too bowed: an anxious, considerate, careworn, flatulent, funny, honest, spry, nearly-78-year-old man with most of his marbles intact, who left his loved ones wanting more.

JULIAN, age 77 when he passed, 5′10.5″, 148 lbs.; blue eyes; red hair thinned to white wisps; this garment-center retiree was a kind and compassionate man who had difficulty communicating the depth of his feelings to his family, but loved to tell them stories, virtually all of which occurred either on a Brooklyn ballfield or near the Mendlesham Airfield, northeast of London, where he served as an air force mechanic with the 34th Bomb Group during World War II. When his eldest son was nursing a broken heart, he related a never-before-told tale: "She was a red-haired girl from Ipswich. I was only 19, just about your age. Two months later, she fell for another Yank, a pilot and an officer who outranked, outgunned, and outmanned a staff sergeant like me." The pilot flew one of the B-17s that Julian serviced, the same one that gave him a gash above the eye from a propeller [we'd often heard the "propeller" story]. After an honorable discharge, he wrote a few letters overseas, but the girl never wrote back. A few years later, he met his future wife, Marion, on a blind date. "And that was that," Julian said.

If it's true but sad that a father must die before his son can finally walk like a man, then the master plan is amiss. The entire structure is built on a fragile, faulty foundation. The basic plot is in need of a new twist.

Yet I become living proof of the adage's truth.

When Dad died, so did my love affair with loss. That elegiac philosophy may have been a fine one in theory, but it was a lot less appealing in actual, here-today-gone-later-today reality. If you spend all your time missing what's gone, you lose out on most of the pleasures that remain.

Some of my ruminations become rueful, not about lost life (Dad's or mine), but regarding the speed with which it goes. Years ago, there was some comfort, a little solace, and at least one consolation: youth. It absolved you of responsibility, excused your impertinence, and even immunized you from disease and prosecution.

I haven't been young in quite a while, but that hasn't stopped me from continuing to think, dream, and live like a

LEE ROBERT SCHREIBER

man half my age. That life of Peter Pan–like denial can only take you so far, and I have reached that point.

I am growing up.

Of my many mournful musings, I have few regrets. My dad had a relatively good, long run. And, after a lifetime of non-communicative fits and starts, he and I ultimately left little unsaid. One curious thought, however, is impossible to shake: My father will never know my wife (or child).

There are no viable contenders, and I've never felt an overwhelming desire to be hitched and/or saddled (though the desire for offspring seems to be spawning). But the mere inkling that I'll never share such a belated miracle with my dear ol' dad makes me maudlin beyond measure.

A long time ago, I did have the opportunity to hook up legally with the college girlfriend who'd been at the heart of so much sturm, drang, passion, and lovesick paeans. But, for a variety of reasons, I passed.

I'll Marry You Tomorrow, but Let's Honeymoon Tonight

A year after graduation—and about as long since we'd broken up—my presumptive soul mate called my office (cubicle) and asked me to dinner. I assumed it was to tell me that she was getting married.

As we were finishing our appetizers, she said: "I want to marry *you.*"

We stayed together for another year—during which,

for the most part, she was on her best behavior. Until: it was time to play some hardball.

She started with a few wild threats, and kept me off balance with several conciliatory curveballs. Her final pitch, however, was masterful.

With her parents away on vacation for two weeks, she moved into my basement apartment with the expressed goal to anticipate my every culinary, sexual, and emotional need.

"Oh, Honey, that was so-o-o wonderful," she purred to me on the linoleum kitchen floor—ten minutes after she'd met me at the door in nothing but high heels, perhaps a half hour before we'd be digging into the homemade lasagna baking just a few feet away.

No one could say that I wasn't given fair warning. Our two-week idyll was designated from the get-go as our last test, a final look-how-wonderful-life-together-could-be session before my decision was due.

"If you can't make up your mind after 14 days of living together," she said, "then you never will. And I'll have no choice but to leave you for good."

I knew she'd make good on her vow, having already left on numerous occasions, and sometimes when there was no occasion at all. But I thought we had an understanding, due to our many separations precipitated by her many betrayals. Though she swore her youthful indiscretions were behind her, she did acknowledge that it might take a while before I might reasonably be able to trust her again.

"Take all the time you need, Honey," she said to me when we first got back together, "as long as it doesn't take *too* long."

"Time" was one of those loose doctrines forever open to interpretation.

This was how I saw it: *You're born, you get married, you die.* If you eliminate that middle part, maybe you postpone the inevitable end.

Hey, it's just a joke. And surely I could not have been that permanently damaged in heart or mind to believe such nonsense. But I was genuinely torn: How could I actually marry *her*, end up in the same household till death did us part . . . this woman who broke my heart again and again . . . and again? (*Why* I kept coming back is a topic addressed later.) I may have loved her, but I did not trust her. And, even at 24, I knew that marriage was primarily an act of trust.

On what would be our final night together, she quietly but firmly said: "Commit to me, or I'll find someone who will."

I didn't. She did.

In light of my unaltered marital status, she obviously made the right move. And while I haven't really second-guessed my decision, here's another line to make grown men weep: *I never saw her naked again.*

Better Off Without a Wife

I chose not to tie the knot back then because:

- I was too young (24);

- We'd spent three of our six years apart (mainly due to her faithlessness);

- I mistakenly assumed, based on our history, that I'd soon get another opportunity;

- I thought, as a would-be writer, it would be a better career move to learn to live with loss as a richly textured abstract notion and constant ache, rather than actually reside with it (her).

How Long Has This Been Going On?

I don't know if it was a *writer* thing or a *guy* thing, or maybe just a born *sentimentalist's* predisposition, but the seasons' brutally quick progression (or regression) has been a lifelong concern and predominant theme. I've always been a sucker for any cinematic, theatrical, literary, and musical work that could wring the pathos out of a variation of the here-today-gone-later-today theme.

For the first 19 years of life, I watched, read, and listened to the great works with great, but dispassionate, interest. The words, pictures, and music may have moved me, but they didn't always reach me. Then Sarah came along, left me, and I became passionately attuned to every (heretofore-buried, now-exposed) synapse and nerve ending.

I was especially proud of the fact that I'd never cried at a movie. That changed with *Love Among the Ruins*—a goddamn *television* movie—starring Katharine Hepburn (as the wealthy, headstrong widow and aging grande dame of the London stage who's sued for breach of promise by a young gigolo) and Sir Laurence Olivier (Edwardian England's greatest barrister, who's asked to defend—as it turns out—his great lost love).

I started choking up at first sight of Hepburn, the ostensibly oblivious and assuredly self-absorbed actress, (re)uniting with Olivier, the obviously still-besotted and self-conscious lawyer. I started leaking when Hepburn finally admitted that she fondly and equally remembered their affair. And I sobbed again at the end for mostly personal reasons: I was in the midst of breaking up—for the umpteenth-and-last time—with my college sweetheart of six years. No doubt I was imagining us in, oh, 35 or 40 years, touchingly reconnecting after concluding the better portion of our adult lives.

Got to Go Back

The older you get, the less preoccupied you are with thematic, theoretical, and metaphorical matters, and the more you concentrate on literal, tangible, unadorned evidence. Making my (figurative) turn on the back nine, and having lost my mentor–caddie–swing doctor–cart driver and playing partner (Dad) and adoring face in the crowd (Grace), I face perhaps my last, best shot at, let's call it, happiness.

Certain truths have become unassailably self-evident: If I am ever going to have a sporting chance of finding a newer, truer, or equally soulful mate—or even come to terms with a perennially solitary fate—I have to seek, find, and confront the genesis of my all-too-human condition. No, not God, Allah, Jehovah, or any Higher Power. This mystery would unravel on terra firma, and most likely on a patch of suburban ground inhabited by a certain wife and mother. No, not my poor grieving Ma. You know who. *Her.* The long-departed college sweetheart who unwittingly holds a key piece to the "commitment" puzzle (and who may also possess a chunk of my manhood as well).

18

Besides, as Grandma Rose (1900–96) used to say, "It couldn't hurt."

My grandmother, however, was nuts—briefly but certifiably institutionalized in her teens, and then again as a 41-year-old mother of two teenaged children, and electro-shocked into permanent sanguinity. I, with a much milder predisposition toward melancholia, have no doubt that it can—and will—hurt plenty.

In the past, I have avoided the heart of all matters because I feared pain, rejection, and the perception of appearing weak and foolish. But after Dad passed away, so did many of these fears. The worst has occurred, and I am still standing. Nothing can hurt me as deeply. I am a big boy who can handle anything, even the truth. I *require* it.

Once and for all, I am prepared to ask the most brutal, potentially face-losing questions, the answers to which I'd previously been too scared to consider:

- How often, if ever, does she ("the one") think of me (and in what context)?
- Are my remembrances of the relationship accurate, or have I been clinging to self-protective delusions?
- Are we soul mates?
- If so, how could she have moved on to someone else so quickly, so apparently easily and painlessly?
- Could a man in love with his own youth find beauty in a woman who's no longer young?
- Is love blind, or just in need of a new prescription?
- Did this idealization of youth (and the perfect girl who accompanied it) permit or compel me to let go of

other women in my past that I could've loved or perhaps did love? (If so, how could I track *them* down?)

- How would she—the up-till-now purported *one* truest
  love—respond to my intrusion into her life . . . with
  dismissive laughter, tears, annoyance, and/or a restraining order?

- And, finally, can I parlay a first-person account of this
  experience into a book/movie/reality TV show?

We have not laid eyes on each other for a dozen years (and had
not laid hands, or any other parts, for more than twice as
long). I am not precisely sure how encountering her after all
this time will bring me closer to closure, but I've tried everything else:

- long-term relationships;
- one-night stands;
- friends of friends;
- friends of relatives;
- relatives of friends;
- friends;
- relatives;
- therapy;
- analysis;
- recreational medication;
- professional medication;
- how-to seminars;
- self-help literature . . .

And none of it—none of *them*—has brought me to the depths of affection and intimacy I had for this one young girl way back when.

Pathetic or Romantic? You make the call.

In no time, I have my nod from the gods: My younger brother, Keith, attends family day at the nursery school where Zachary, his youngest child (my nephew and godson), is matriculated. Keith bends down to tie Zach's shoelaces, while his wife introduces him to the school director.

"Keith?" says the director, a darkly attractive woman in her forties. "Do you have a brother named Lee?"

Keith looks up. He hasn't seen the woman since puberty, but he immediately recognizes her.

"Sarah!" he says.

Two weeks later, I make the call (actually I *e-mail* her).

2

Sentimental Journey

Where the Boys Are

"Schmuck! You did *what*!?"

The Boys, nearly to a man, are aghast. I am surprised, considering that we've avidly discussed these very sorts of issues for years. I thought Boys' Night Out—collectively and individually—would be a lot more supportive of my initiative.

"It's one thing to riff nostalgic about your old underwear," says Andy. "It's quite another to root around in the drawer searching for the actual pair."

> **ANDY,** 49, 5′11″, 182 lbs.; shaved-bald head; brown-haired goatee; blue eyes; after years of trying, the 36-year-old wife he often refers to as "a superstar" gave birth to fraternal twin girls. "Poetic justice," the quasi-chauvinistic orthopedic surgeon admits. Still, he says, he gets a twinge in his gut whenever he sees or speaks to Sari, a former high school girlfriend who's been married to one of his closest childhood pals for more than 20 years.

"You have no idea what you've done!" Gerry yells at me. "Why the hell would you *choose* to pick at the scabs of an old wound?!"

Whoa, chill out, Ger.

Of all the Boys, Gerry is the most vehement and vocal in his opposition to this entire track-her-down-and-confront-her-to-get-closure plan. He is not, I should add, indiscriminately raining on my parade. His own marriage was hampered and ultimately shortened by the looming presence of another "one."

GERRY (short for Geraldo), 5′9″, 162 well-muscled pounds; a 37-year-old fireman who was married at 19. Fifteen years later, he found his wife in bed with her high school sweetheart (the affair had been going on throughout their marriage). Though he dates often, he acknowledges that he'll "never get over it" and he'll "never find another one." Gerry is an empathic guy who tends to get overly involved in the lives of everyone that he knows and likes.

"Hopefully she won't respond to your e-mail," Gerry continues. "If she does, just tell her it was a mistake. Then delete all related messages from your hard drive, and your own memory."

"Gerry's right," Chung says. "No good can come of this—for you, for her, and, above all, for her family." If you recall, Chung is also speaking from painful personal history. "Some things you don't mess with. It's like the *Star Trek* directive, the time-space continuum or whatever. You go back and screw with something or someone from the past, and it can totally change the course of human history. At least the *male* part."

I believe Chung is calling me a [tacky, puerile euphemism for a woman's most private of body parts].

Screw 'em. Not one of them can ease the chill on a winter's

night. Or bring me chicken soup during cold and flu season. Nor is there a man or woman among them who can promise me their undying support, approval, and love . . .

Chung is right; I *am* a [woman's most private part].

But it is too late to reverse time. I have already, in a real and metaphorical sense, *booked* passage on the way-gone machine . . . the wheels are spinning backward . . . the calendar days are peeling away and flying off . . .

The old songs are starting to echo . . . and I am tumbling ass-over-teakettle in a nostalgic haze of fogged memory, second-hand pot smoke, and the exhaust fumes of a vinyl-topped Buick Wildcat . . .

Unchained Melody

My father and I drove two hours from our suburban Long Island home to a picturesque liberal arts college in up-state New York. He helped me get settled in the dorm and meet my two roommates; then we walked around the campus and into town, where he filled me up with some supplies and the last meal in months I'd consume outside a cafeteria.

I could count on one hand and two toes the full days that Dad and I ever spent together, just the two of us. This was one of the fullest. It ended all too quickly, accompanied by the typically awkward father-son moment in the parking lot. We'd never been a particularly demonstrative family, yet it seemed perfectly natural at that moment to lean in for the "guy" hug (body positioned to avoid package-to-package contact and a couple of quick back taps); I even added a peck on his cheek.

Sad as I may have been to see the old man go, I was ecstatic to be out from under my parents' roof, thumb, and apparently arbitrary list of rules and regulations. At long last, I could breathe—except for the Buick's faint, lingering exhaust fumes—September air that was free and clear.

Ah, to be on one's own—or the middle-class equivalent, in which mom and dad shell out for room, board, and tuition, and you get to make all day-to-day decisions regarding sleeping, eating, partying, and studying.

Certainly some attention had to be paid toward school or I'd flunk out, which would then be followed by several serious consequences:

- an abrupt end to the free ride;
- loss of a student deferment;
- reclassification of draft status;
- conscription into the armed services;
- a shave;
- a haircut;
- one-way transport to Southeast Asia.

"Wow I didn't know that you *nearly* served in Vietnam!" says Gerry.

Chung, our youngest Boy, chirps in, "Man, that would've been so-o-o cool."

Andy and I—teenaged Boomers in harm's way during this

period—each give the callow pair a solid whack to their respective noodles.

"Oww!!"

"What the—!?!"

"You guys think jungle warfare is *cool*!?" says Andy, whose first year of college was the last of the war. "You [Chung], take this bayonet!" He hands him a steak knife. "And here's yours." Gerry gets a butter knife. "Now, fight to the death."

For a long moment, we don't know if Andy is kidding or what (he is), but Phil (a slightly older boomer with a graduate school deferment) cuts the tension by giving them extra spoons and napkins. Turning to me, he says: "See, I always said Vietnam *was* a picnic."

Too Soon Gone

I hated serving any authority figures, especially those in the educational system—with the rules, the tedium, the dutiful behavior of my classmates, the relentless pursuit of good grades, the irrational dread of a black mark on one's permanent record. My blasé attitude toward higher achievement baffled and irritated teachers, guidance counselors, fellow students, and parents, especially my own.

"You have so much potential," they said.

Nothing gave me such pleasure as to hear, and to know, that I had these vast resources of resourcefulness to tap if and when I chose. It was a comfort to consider that there was lots of time in which I could still buckle down, apply myself, and/or commit to a plan of action. But, even back then, a part of me knew that reveling too long in unlimited potential, or refusing to limit my choices, could lead to unfulfilled youthful promise(s). *Someday Soon* can become, in what seemed like a few dozen eye blinks, *Too Soon Gone*.

I didn't need a higher education to learn that life was short, and I intended to live every semester as if it was my last. No matter what I'd be doing with the next four years, I knew that I would not be sucking up to some second-rate professor *or* cowering in some Vietnamese shitstorm.

Just in case, though, I needed a hedge. So, in the pursuit of peace (and, secondarily, as a good place to meet free-thinking, loose-loving, bra-optional co-eds), I headed to the student hall building on the bucolic Old Campus quad for my first undergraduate anti-war meeting.

In retrospect, it was the defining moment in what was to become, up to that point, the most eventful week of my life.

Student Demonstration Time

Sunday 7:30 PM

The upcoming march in Poughkeepsie was the primary topic on the Student Moratorium Committee agenda, but I could not keep my eyes off of two young beauties who were situated on either side of the room; and who, I'd soon discover, resided at polar ends of the class's student body: 19-year-old Pearl R., a stunning, milk-fed blonde from rural Allegheny County; and 17-year-old Sarah B., dark-haired, equally comely and shapely, from the county of Queens.

Though I'd soon fall madly, deeply, and possibly truly with one, and would eventually sleep with the other many years later, neither girl took much notice of me, even after I was named the lone freshman on the steering committee.

"What's their story?" I asked George, the fifth-year senior who led the committee and who served briefly as my mentor. He basically dismissed the twin objects of my desire as "flighty and not-too-bright," more intent on finding husbands than effecting meaningful societal change.

> **GEORGE,** 23-year-old, fifth-year senior, 6', 145 lbs.; brown shoulder-length hair often tied in a ponytail; a classic underachiever with a huge chip on his shoulder who might've seen a kindred spirit in me. We often stayed up late in his flophouse room, drinking cheap port, discussing disparate political philosophies (early vs. late Malcolm X; Machiavelli vs. Rousseau; Edmund Burke vs. Che Guevara). A month after the Poughkeepsie march, he asked me to work on his documentary, a "manual for organizing unions." After screening early footage, I told him: "I don't get the significance of urinating on the boxcars." "Bourgeois asshole!" he said, banishing me forever. Next I heard, he'd dropped out of school to live, briefly, with his Berkeley girlfriend, who soon left him for a member of the Weather Underground [a radical group of militants intent on overthrowing the establishment with violent acts of "strategic sabotage"]. Years later, I recognized him walking purposefully across an avenue in midtown Manhattan; he was dressed in a three-piece suit and lugging a huge briefcase. He did not see me.

I Know There's an Answer

The last you heard, I had e-mailed *the* object of my longstanding desire and affection. This was the entire message:

From: Lee S
To: Sarah F [her married initial]
Sent: Wednesday 5:04 PM
Subject: Reunion

```
You might recall that we attended the same
college a long, long time ago. We dated for
several years, and then went our separate ways.
My brother mentioned that he ran into you
recently, and that you're co-director of a
large private school. None of this information
should come as a great surprise to you. This
note, however, might. Surprise!
Here's another one: I'd like to get together
with you. Soon.
My intent is strictly professional: I'd like to
talk to you about a project that I'm working on.
So, how 'bout it? Breakfast, lunch or dinner?
Some time in the next two weeks?
Please let me know if and when you can meet
me. It should be interesting.
I look forward to hearing from, and seeing, you
soon. Thanks.
Lee
```

"You're delusional!" Gerry rages. "You can't distinguish past from present, real from imagined."

Admittedly the note isn't my strongest creative work. But *delusional?* That seems a bit extreme. Besides, the content is secondary. My main goal is to pique her interest.

"I thought the tone was just right—not too cool, and not too much like a wiseass," says my gal pal Beth. Finally, an ally. "And by being a little vague, you've intrigued her. As opposed to: 'I've often thought about you during these past two decades . . . and oh, by the way, I'm writing a book about our relationship.' If I ever received that message from an old boyfriend, I'd immediately change the locks and unlist my phone."

Beth, an ex-girlfriend of mine, often provides balance and perspective—for me and the rest of the Boys. Throughout our 13-year friendship, she has often joked about me being "the one that got away." When we dated, she was the first person to suggest that maybe I needed to resolve a few things with Sarah before I could get serious with somebody else (like, for example, her). Of all the Boys' Night Out regulars, Beth is easily the most supportive, expansive, and complimentary.

"I'm proud of you," she says. "I think it's a brave thing to risk utter humiliation and rejection by trying to bring some long-needed closure to this chapter of your life. And besides," she adds, "it'll make a great book."

Well, at this point, the likelihood of closing an emotional chapter or a book deal is looking grim. Because: After four full days, Sarah has not responded.

Thursday had come and gone. Friday rose and fell. Saturday peaked and valleyed. Sunday dawned and dusked.

Not a word.

Sounds of Silence

I don't deal well with silence. I tend to fill it up with my most insecure, gloom-packed, worst-case imaginings. If I contact someone and they don't immediately reply, I wonder: What's the matter? And then, as more time goes by without rejoinder or acknowledgment, I think: What's the matter with me?

What *is* the matter? I come from a loving (if undemonstrative) middle-class family. I'm not damaged in any visible way. I harbor no great envy or regret. Yet, born or made, it seems that I've always been predisposed toward a melancholy or elegiac streak that sometimes somehow gums up much of my objective thought processing.

What's the deal with that? How is it that some folks seem innately carefree and confident, fully able to enact positively self-fulfilling lives, while others like me struggle to avoid the manifestation of our blackest musings? As mentioned, I've tried:

- short-term therapy;
- long-term therapy, including analysis (four times a week for three years at a cut-rate cost of $8 per session);
- medication (for depression, anxiety, and insomnia).

And none of these measures has brought me much relief from the unaffirmative, impugning, nullifying voices in my head (figuratively speaking). So when for four full days there is no retort to my invitation, I am feeling quite per—

Oh, screw it.

Who am I kidding with this fake suspense?

Of course, she responds.

Of course, she agrees to see me.

(She'd just taken a few days off. After a long weekend off, she returned to the office, logged on, and promptly sent the following:)

From: Sarah F
Sent: Monday 9:43 AM

```
Well this certainly came as a surprise.
Sure I'll meet you. You definitely have my
curiosity up. Getting to the city in the next
week or two is a bit difficult for me (both
kids are coming home from college) but here are
a few possibilities: this Friday evening,
Saturday afternoon or next Monday night. Let me
know what your schedule is like. Oh, for the
record, I'm "THE" director, not the co-director
(not that I have any ego issues or anything).
See you soon,
Sarah
```

So there it is. And there I go . . . back to my fully functional, chronically low-grade disquietude . . . and back to those other voices *outside* my head.

Do Nothing till You Hear from Me

"Well, maybe you can now put this whole thing to bed—figuratively speaking, of course—once and for all," Robert says.

> **ROBERT,** 39, 6'1", 174 lbs.; thinning blondish crew-cut hair; green eyes; says he's fallen in love only once—and not since his first year of residency at a psychiatric hospital—with Lawrence, a soon-to-be released patient. The two men remained live-in partners until Lawrence—who'd been diagnosed as suffering from bipolar mood disorder with a predisposition toward depression—jumped off their fifth-floor terrace to his death.

"You have to hand it to White Meat," Joseph says, pointing to me with his huge paw. "The rest of y'all—excepting you, Beth—don't have the balls to risk such emotional rejection."

> **JOSEPH**, 46, 6'1", 330 lbs.; brown hair and eyes; hospital aide (and occasional bouncer); a classic inner-city story: dealt drugs in his teens; didn't meet his father till he was about 21; had four kids by two women (none by his ex-wife or current girlfriend). Yet, in his neighborhood, his story is unusual: dropped out of college just six credits shy of graduation ("my biggest regret," he says), but has always worked at good jobs, and has remained emotionally and financially connected to all of his kids; he also cares for his girl-friend of ten years (who wants to marry him, but not necessarily move in with him). "Take the deal, Big Man," we tell him, but he prefers to have a steady mate, yet remain legally single and live alone.
>
> Come to think of it, not a bad deal at all.

Joseph (never Joe or Joey) offers, in his words, the "other, brother" perspective. He is not above using his imposing black presence to get the other "boys"—he has no problem with the supposedly derogatory term—to fall in line with his opinions. Of late, he has been trying to intimidate me: "You will not be sharing any of my stories in your book." (Too late, Big Man.)

If Beth and Joseph are onboard with my quest, the other fellows—with the exception of Gerry—will eventually follow. And sure enough, after another few drinks, they are pretty much slurring and slobbering approval, encouragement, and even envy at the once-in-a-lifetime opportunity I've carved out for myself.

"Way cool," says Chung.

"Should be a helluva ride," says Phil.

"You the man!" says Andy.

But, as usual, it is Beth who cuts through the b.s. with the most insightful question I've yet fielded regarding the upcoming reunion: "What are you going to wear?"

Wednesday 1:30 AM

Wearing my lucky gray-green woolen vest over a black tee shirt, I was alone in the student activities' office, cranking out—literally, on an old mimeo press—leaflets for my two sub-committees (Name-Reading of the War Dead and The All-Night Vigil before the Poughkeepsie March) when the bell to the storefront door tippled, announcing the arrival of two girls who'd shown up to volunteer: Pearl and Sarah. The mother lode for freshman fantasies.

While Pearl peed, Sarah offered me a Marlboro. Before college, I'd never tasted cigarette tobacco, but I'd wisely taken up the habit for this very reason: as a conversation starter with girls.

"Sure, thanks," I said. "I'm still trying to decide if I'm a Marlboro or a Kools man."

"Ah, menthols," she said, which was our entire conversation.

Before I could get an accurate read on either girl (how smart, savvy, or available)—and seeing how there was no real work to be done—both babes bade me a good morning, leaving me to crank out the final versions of my leaflets (and, if I recall, a spectacular noturnal emission during my subsequent REM cycle).

Wednesday 8:30 AM

Red-eyed and lightheaded from about three hours' sleep, I met with the dean of students in his office to discuss our inalienable right to assemble.

I was amazed by the progressive attitude of this college administration, whose authorities shared our views and could not have been nicer in facilitating our activities. (When subsequent actions by our nation's leaders made the seizure of college campuses *de rigueur*, most faculty members gave us the keys—literally—to their offices.)

From: Lee S
Sent: Wednesday 10:37 AM

```
dear sole director,
how 'bout friday nite for dinner? pick a
convenient time per your work & train schedule,
and i'll choose a place.
l
```

From: Sarah F
Sent: Wednesday 2:13 PM

```
I think Friday should be fine. I'll confirm with
you tomorrow. I'm just trying to get in touch
with my prodigal son to see when he's coming
home (he's expected on Thursday). I'll check
the train schedule and let you know the exact
minute of my arrival. Who's paying?
```

From: Lee S
Sent: Wednesday 4:51 PM

```
i thought you had some big job. regardless,
i invited you; so i will of course pick up
the tab.
```

Wednesday 10:40 PM

It was my additional committee duty to preside over the All-Night Vigil's open microphone. Little acquainted with public speaking, I required a few fists of liquid courage. Even less familiar with the effects of Southern Comfort, a syrupy 76-proof concoction favored by Janis Joplin before her premature demise at 27, my head soon began spinning, then the microphone, then the crowd . . .

Thursday 6:30 AM

Dry mouth, pounding head, the chills. So this was the dreaded hangover I'd heard so much about. As best as I could piece together, I'd passed out unconscious in introductory mid-stream, was then carried into the student lounge men's bathroom, where I awakened to several gut-retching explosions—all of which, proud to say, made the bowl—followed by several hours of uninterrupted, semi-delirious, fetal-positioned sleep on the cold, hard tile floor.

From: Sarah F
Sent: Thursday 9:11 AM

My son has confirmed: He is coming home from school on Thursday, so Friday should be fine. Do you have a cell number in case of emergency? Also I need to know where to meet, and how will I recognize you.

From: Lee S
Sent: Thursday 9:32 AM

send regards to your kid. no cell phone—don't believe in 'em. you have my home number if there's a problem. let's meet at nadine's, a low-key, neighborhood place. will you be transporting yourself in the city via cab, bus or subway?
i pretty much look like me, except jowlier, with different glasses and a virtually unrecognizable hairpiece.
i told you this would be fun.

Thursday 9:45 AM

I managed to clamber aboard the bus before it departed for the Poughkeepsie march. When we reached the starting point, I fell queasily into line, though each unsteady step on pavement stirred my unsteady stomach and every irritating chant ("What do we want? Peace! When do we want it? Now!!!") shot fiery spikes into my brain. Adding insult to misery, I spotted both Sarah and Pearl—for me, the prime movers in the anti-war movement—holding hands, respectively, with upperclassmen.

From: Sarah F
Sent: Thursday 3:01 PM

Since you've agreed to pay for dinner (I won't order much), I'll spring for a cab. My train is scheduled to arrive at 5:49. If all goes well, I will see you at Nadine's between 6:15 and 6:30pm. If you need to reach me, here's my cell number [555/555-5555]. I hope it's fun—I don't usually enjoy coming into the city.

From: Lee S
Sent: Friday 10:00 AM

i'll reserve accordingly. (what's with all this money talk?) see you soon.

Friday 9:33 PM

My two roommates had left for the weekend. In preparation for my first college dance, I put the final punctuation to my hair—a dangling comma of forelock—and then addressed my possible wardrobe choices.

The Nearness of You

Friday, 5:04 PM

An hour or so before the re-visitation, I survey the clothes armoire in my tiny Manhattan apartment, and my eyes water with sentiment. No doubt, my emotive outlets, anticipating a surge of uncrossed wires, are primed to overload on contact. But that's not what causes the leakage.

It is the sight of a blue-and-white striped, short-sleeved, cotton-seersucker-polyester-blend shirt that I'd appropriated from my father's collection when—a week after his funeral—my brother and I went through his effects.

My dad lived by a few very basic rules, among them: "Shirt pockets are designed to hold toothpicks—you never know when you'll need one." (An accompanying principle: "When helping yourself to a restaurant's complementary stash, don't make a pig of yourself." So, to double the cache, while also conserving it, our father broke each toothpick *in half*.)

As my brother and I literally picked through the pockets of every shirt in his regular rotation, we found at least three or four wood slivers in each—all in halves. When we were finished, there was a mound of broken sticks piled about three inches high. We could not help but smile through our tears at this characteristically simple, splendid shrine of splinters.

Like my father, I am a creature of habited habits. I tend toward the same few articles of clothing until they wear (or someone throws them) out. On the night I'm convening with that extra-special lady from yore, I need something sartorially special—stylish, flattering, spotless, comfortable, fitted and fitting.

I've been accused by friends and exes of "behaving like a woman" when it comes to choosing the perfect outfit for a particular event. While I have no problem with their gender-based description, I believe it's inaccurate. In my experience, women are more likely to plan ahead, thinking, rethinking, and resolving their wardrobe choices before it's time to actually put them on. I, on the other hand, like to go by feel and mood, to wait and see which way the wind is blowing, so to speak, before I pick and choose.

On this night, my mood dictates the donning of all my favorite (which just happen to be my *newest*) items:

- black wool pants—cuffed, flat front, perfect break— displaced from my Italian-cut three-button, single-breasted suit jacket (the entire suit might be a bit much for this occasion);
- black silk (the good, substantial kind, not that shiny, flimsy crepe crap) vented shirt, over a white tee shirt for contrast. (Also juxtaposing the all-black formality is a tasteful pattern of tiny martini glasses and musical notes subtly embroidered in beige on either side of the shirt's buttons);
- black socks with beige flecks peeking out from the tops of my black mid-cut shoe-boot lace-ups;
- black cashmere-wool overcoat (unbuttoned);
- and, capping off the fun-funereal outfit, my new favorite watch—a 27-year-old, black-faced Bucherer watch, which I'd also lifted from my father's "estate."

The watch indicates **6:05**. I have ten minutes till the appointed time, but need only five to reach the restaurant.

Friday 10:33 PM

Suitably outfitted in patched dungarees (that's what we used to call jeans), forest-green short-sleeved pocket tee and a long-sleeved light-blue workshirt layered under a brown corduroy jacket, I began the six-minute walk from my dorm to the hall. (It's been neither confirmed nor denied, but I lay claim to the colored-tee-under-collared-shirt look; prior to my donning, the only suitable under wear was white).

Friday 10:39 PM

I stood in front of the cafeteria, taking a minute to steel myself. A few deep breaths from the still, chilled fall air mingled with burnt, stray particles of primo marijuana.

Primed, stoked, and second-hand smoked, I stepped onto the dining-cum-dance hall and prepared to face the music.

3

Strangers in the Night

Friday, 6:10 PM

I am seated at the best table in the house with a view of the door. No sign of her, but it is early.

"No thanks," I say, waving off the waiter's request for my drink order. "I'm waiting for someone."

I Saw Her Standing There

Friday 10:41 PM

Inside the darkened cafeteria, my eyes took a few seconds to adjust and then focused on a curvaceous girl dressed in a white peasant blouse, long dungaree (denim) skirt and high black boots lazily dancing with some friends.

She was about ten yards away, so I couldn't see her face, but there was something in the way she moved. She turned. My stomach did a little flip. It was her. You know

42

the one. No, not beautiful, blond Pearl. The other one: the dark-haired, 17-year-old, second-semester freshwoman named Sarah.

She caught my eye and smiled. Her smile was so genuine and warm—nothing like my usual self-protective, shit-eating grin—that I couldn't help but respond in kind. Before I was conscious of any other physical reaction, I'd instinctively started to walk in her direction. When I reached her, the music was too loud for discussion— I think it was the Allman Brothers, probably "Whipping Post"—so I leaned in and pressed two fingers to my lips, pantomiming the universal sign for cigarette.

She pointed to the "No Smoking" sign on the cafeteria wall. I threw down the fake butt and stomped it out. She laughed. Emboldened, I pointed to the floor and twisted spastically (the universal symbol for dancing).

She laughed again, a full, throaty peal. The next moment, though it might strain credulity, we were gyrating in sync to Van Morrison's "Moondance": *"Well it's a marvelous night for a moondance, with the stars up above in your eyes, a fantabulous night to make romance 'neath the cover of October skies . . . You know the night's magic seems to whisper and hush, and all the soft moonlight seems to shine in your blush . . . "* (Van's "Crazy Love" would eventually become "our" song.)

Friday 11:01 PM

Four minutes and thirty-five seconds later, we were swaying to a different tune. Oh-so-slowly. The song? I don't have the foggiest recollection. I do remember that her hair smelled of vanilla and that our bodies kept inching tighter and closer until we were cheek to cheek, chest to breast, and I worried that my oak-hard boner would soon become an embarrassment. She seemed lost in the music, eyes closed, her head gently resting on my shoulder . . . and yet, I could almost swear that she ever-so-slightly, yet oh-so-delicately and even teasingly rubbed against it, and I became greatly concerned that I might squeeze off a pant full. But the song ended, and we eased to a safe stop.

"Let's get some air," she said, taking my hand.

Friday, 6:13 PM

It is raining outside—a raw, windy evening in early spring—and I wonder if she is having trouble getting a cab.

Moondance

Saturday 12:08 AM

The autumn air was crisp and clear. The sky was starry and cloudless. The immediate world was ours, and we covered every bit of available ground, freely sharing our life stories, such as they were at 18 and 17, respectively. I listened to her talk, taking it all in . . .

"I was a change-of-life baby," she said, "with two much older brothers. My mother's a dear, though a little ditzy at times. But my father . . . " She paused and grinned mischievously. "Well, he can come across as cranky and intimidating."

How so?

"He rarely smiles. Plus, he sort of resembles the blind guy in *The Great Escape*."

Donald Pleasence, I said.

She seemed impressed.

"Yeah, well," she laughed. "Few people would describe him as pleasant. But you just have to know how to play him. I'm definitely Daddy's little girl."

I was impressed. She was funny with a little sarcastic edge. She was obviously not flighty or dimwitted in the least. She seemed pretty damn smart to me, especially when I learned that she was already in her second semester while barely two months past her 17th birthday. She had a preternatural presence about her; she could easily have been 20 or 21 years old.

Oh, and one more thing: Remember the guy she held hands with at the peace march?

"What a schmuck," she said. "He just wanted one thing."

I, on the other hand, wanted everything.

Friday, 6:14 PM

Believe me, I don't want to keep up the rapid cross-cutting of time frames. But I figure she'll be arriving any minute, and I prefer to be alone, maybe for the last time, with *my* memories. . . .

This Could Be the Start of Something Big
Saturday 12:55 AM

When it was my turn to impress her with my depth and breadth, I tried to cram everything into one breath: "Hated high school . . . love sports—baseball, softball, football, and soccer . . . and games of skill—poker, backgammon, hearts . . . read lots of fiction—Fitzgerald, Updike, J.P. Donleavy, Ken Kesey . . . some poetry, too—e.e. cummings, Dylan Thomas, Yeats . . . yeah, do some writing of my own . . . haven't declared a major yet, but probably English . . . my great passion, though, is music, all kinds—Tom Rush, Charles Lloyd, Brian Wilson, Nina Simone, Babatunde Olatunji, Sinatra, Satchmo, Rossini, Blossom Dearie, Robert Johnson, and Loudon Wainwright III—the more wrenching or wry the better. . . . My father's in the garment business—a good man, a true *mensch*, but a little distant and withholding. . . . Ma's a force of nature—tough, no-nonsense, independent, she can't wait for her kids to grow up. . . . You'd like my 15-year-old sister—though, to me, she's a huge pain in the ass. . . . Little brother's definitely my pride and joy—he's eight, smart, funny, adorable. . . . Me? Gemini. You don't believe in that stuff, do you? Though, come to think of it, my mother, sister, and you are all Virgos. What do you make of that? . . . "

For a poker player who rarely showed his cards, I couldn't stop my yap from *telling* everything. It must've been nervousness, eagerness, anxiety . . .

"Relax," she said, touching my arm. "We have plenty of time."

And the damnedest thing: I shut up.

I guess I believed her.

Friday, 6:14 PM

I shake free of these reflections when a speeding cab splashes water on the window next to my table. In its wake, the restaurant's door flings out wide, accompanied by a loud male voice flinging curses. A woman trails, appearing as if she would prefer to be elsewhere. First date, I'm guessing.

Some Enchanted Evening

First dates are rarely memorable. They're usually last dates. *Bon Soir* and *Arrivederci*. Then, on that rarest of occasions, there are some enchanted evenings when you just know "This Could Be the Start of Something Big." If you have any sort of sappy streak, you savor the little mundane moments, knowing they will all too quickly pass.

I have spent more hours than I care to admit savoring retrospective moments. I glance down again at Dad's—at *my*—timepiece: **6:16 PM.** It seems about time to wrap up these reveries . . .

Saturday 3:41 AM

After dancing, walking, talking, and making out through the night, we ended up in my dorm room. We talked and kissed until the sun came up. Then, too pooped to purse another syllable or smooch, or even to climb up to my top bunk, we crashed on my roommate's bottom bed. Fully clothed, wrapped in each other's arms, we slept together. Just that. Nothing more.

We saw each other the next day, and the next.

After a week or so, we referred to each other as girl-friend and boyfriend.

Though it would be two months until we'd make, and profess, undying love, we both knew this was *it*—something special and lasting.

I no longer needed a wing man. She would be the one watching my back, and I'd be happily scratching hers.

Friday, 6:17 PM

Of her many fine qualities, I cannot recall if punctuality was one of them. But she'd written "between 6:15 and 6:30," so I probably have a few minutes left for a few mental notes . . .

- What if we'd never met?
- What if I'd never seen her until the moment that she walks through that door?
- Would I still find her beautiful?

The Look of Love

Did I mention that she was gorgeous, a dead ringer for Ava Gardner, Jacqueline Bisset, Jennifer Connelly, Natalie Portman . . . you fill in the darkest, sexiest, most luminous siren of the day. Mostly, though, she reminded me of Annette Funicello, the sultry Mousketeer who embodied the first full-blooming female fantasy for many men born in the 1950s.

And while initially I may have been drawn to her stunning appearance, that's not what made me stay. There was much more to it, and her, than a few lush curves and some skin-deep, bone-structural similarity to Annette Funicello or any-one else.

For starters, it was her look.

More precisely, it's *my* look: what I find appealing in a woman. And the qualities that attract me are not necessarily physical in nature, though their manifestation might include how she:

- walks, laughs, and squints;
- crosses her legs;
- flicks a piece of lint off of someone's arm;
- twirls her hair absent-mindedly when lost in thought.

And, to cap it all off, our sensibilities were in sync on politics, religion, and humor. We shared non-negotiable traits such as playfulness, anti-authoritarianism, and a deep connection to family. Passions ran equally deep with our love of music, movies, travel, and sex (though she was a virgin when we met and I . . . well, we'll get to that).

But, in the end, who can really say what attracts two people? Maybe it's:

- an Oedipal thing that reminds you (in a non-creepy) way of your mom or dad;
- a pheromone phenomenon of mutual chemistry that inexplicably links you;
- an instinctual sense of something so right;
- an indeterminate familiarity, leading you to feel as if you've known this person all your life (or, if you believe in such things, a prior one).

Friday, 6:18 PM

Where was I? Oh, yeah:

- Would I still be attracted to her today?
- Had the situation been different, and we met tonight for the first time ever, would there be something sufficiently compelling about her to propel me past my fearful diffidence and approach her?

Come and Get It

I've never been the kind of guy who could walk up to a disinterested stranger and initiate a conversation.

I've always been too mindful of being hurt, or rejected, and/or appearing foolish. (As a poker player who knows the odds, I rarely make a move unless my estimated chance of success—factoring in my biorhythmic and intoxication levels, her body language and the moon's rotation, all calculated at warp speed—exceed 76.8 percent, my lifetime winning percentage at poker.)

Invariably I justify my inaction with stock rationales such as:

- ⇩ Why bother. She's way out of my league.
- ⇩ Under that form-fitting dress, you just know she's sporting a cellulite-spackled ass with dimples big enough to hide a circus troupe.
- ⇩ What's with the purple nail polish? I'll bet she's a Wicca priestess who must make her monthly quota of man-monkey transformations.

Like many naturally shy, self-conscious people, I typically over-compensate with a seemingly self-possessed confidence often perceived as arrogance. Sometimes, the effect of feigned cock-surety borders on imperiousness. At any public gathering, you can usually identify the most anxious, self-doubting individu-als by their inordinately deadpan, above-it-all and bored-looking faces (as differentiated from plastic-surgery victims who paid for that look).

This is what fear does to us all, or at least to those hypersen-sitive types who overthink the many ways in which they (we) could be hurt, rejected and/or made to appear foolish.

What about all the shameless guys and gals who sidle right up to someones at museums, cocktail parties, grocery stores? They're shot down every day of their lives, yet they just brush themselves off and get right back into the sidle. (These men and women have ended up, throughout the history of time, as the most successful individuals on earth.)

What is it they have that we don't have?

Possibly sociopath personalities. More likely, though, they don't take everything personally. They realize it's a numbers game, and even the greatest swingers fail 70 percent of the time. They don't mind striking out, and who really cares what a group of strangers think about you anyway? And why would you allow *anyone* else to prevent you from pursuing your every goal . . . ?

Friday, 6:19 PM

"Yes," I tell the waiter on his second pass through my station. "I will have a drink—vodka martini stright-up with a twist, please."

(That seemed a lot longer than one minute, no? And, if it

seems like I've processed a lot of material in a very short time, remember: I have lived with this information for quite a long while. It should also come as no surprise, then, that I have a definite opinion regarding "love at first sight.")

Love at First Sight

I believe that the concept does exist, but only in hindsight. Think about it. Think about all those times that Lust, Attraction, and Chemistry were mistaken for the real thing, only to be dashed upon the shoals of despair when you realized that your nearly beloved had, for example:

- a high, whiny voice that only dogs or dolphins could abide;
- an eighth-grade education, much of it self-taught;
- wrong-headed, long-winded opinions about anything and everything.

You try to forget about the ones who got away, all the many ones you initially thought were *the* one, but who over time, proved to be 14th or 32nd on the long road to Disappointment and Disillusionment. You forget almost all of those near-missus and misters in your massive dating portfolio because to remember them is much too painful. Because if you *can* forget, then you'll retain the human, fervid hope that your next instant connection will be the one and only.

Look at Love at First Sight (metaphorically) as the Swiss army of handy-dandy, opposable-thumb-operated implements that not only cuts open a can of worms, it also tries to pin down the writhing, slippery little buggers struggling to break free. And it functions as a barometer, an odometer, a two-way mirror, and a wood-burning hearth. If used correctly, it can transform hope and yearning into a connective bond that no gun, sword, pen, stick, or stone can dent and rent asunder. It even comes with its own directions: *If, say, book follows cover, and all subjective criteria are met, you could perhaps maybe possibly probably almost assuredly fall in love with this person . . .*

Friday, 6:21 PM

I hear a car splash up to the curb. Another flash of yellow cab. I will myself not to peek. If it is her, I don't want a partial fleeting image. I want to take in all of her at once.

I fell in love with a girl when she turned out to be mostly as I'd imagined, the text of the book jibing closely with a cover that advertised:

📖 "I'm smart, so you better keep up."

The restaurant door brightly tipples on opening.

📖 "I love to laugh, but only if it's funny."

It is her. She still has *the* look. A second later, we lock eyes. There is no turning back. (Final question to self: Am I on the brink of enlightenment, or doomed to eternal damnation?)

Oh, jeez, should I hug her? Kiss her? (Definitely not on the mouth.) Shake her hand?

📖 "I will continue to surprise you."

Get a grip. Calm down. Relax. Above all, be honest and open. And don't forget: Life is short; it'll be over soon.

📖 "You can trust me."

Even a fool knows, however, that *looks* can be deceiving.

I've Got a Feeling

At 18, I had nearly been convinced that romantic love was a myth, that only a very few couples (maybe my own parents in their own non-demonstrative way) were blessed with such fortune, and that, factoring in my youthful insecurities and fears, I could never be among the chosen ones. But, after only a few months with Sarah, I was pretty sure that I had found my one and only soul mate.

Friday, 6:23 PM

I am still grappling with that possibility. She sees me and smiles. I stand and wait.

4

Until the Real Thing Comes Along

Will the Circle Be Unbroken?

"Don't expect too much," Beth cautions during an emergency one-on-one Boy-Girl Night Out session convening three days before my dinner with Sarah.

Beth and I haven't dated for 13 years (and fornicated for 12), but she is my go-to pal when it comes to sounding off and trying to suss out the nuances of male-female dynamics.

"She'll probably acknowledge your special relationship," Beth says, "and tell you that she remembers you fondly, even that you were her first love. But, she'll likely also say, 'I've moved on with my life, and I think it's time that that you do, too.'"

Beth also raises the plausible specter of a more severe backlash: "She might have some real anger toward *you*, and take the opportunity to remind you what a thumb-sucking commitment-phobe you were back then. She might even say: 'You had your chance, and you blew it. Have a nice life, loser.'"

Loser?

"All kidding—and book premises—aside," says Beth, "what do you really expect to happen at this get-together?"

Really?

Dream Lover

In the fly-by-night network of Nod where I woolgathered, I had subliminally experienced various reunion scenarios with Sarah. They weren't recurrent dreams as much as they were a series of subconscious-reality episodes that unfolded in a non-sequential narrative arc over the past several years.

I knew that these dreams were only in my head, but there was a pinch-me palpability to them. And during long stretches when my sleep cycle was disrupted or blocked, I could swear that I was experiencing a secret half-life.

Like most dramas "ripped from the headlines . . . based on a true story . . . or inspired by actual events," my dream sequences were influenced but not bound by the few facts I knew about Sarah: long married, with two children, living in a suburb near where I grew up, running a private school.

On any given night, supposable characters, plotlines, and locations would cherry-pick from about a dozen dramatically plausible narratives, usually adding a fanciful twist or two. For example, I conjured Sarah as:

- single and 21;
- single and 45;

- a middle-aged mother of from one to five biological and/or adopted children;
- married, divorced, or widowed;
- fulfilling various custodial arrangements of guardianship;
- living in any one of a dozen exotic locales (Zihuatanejo, Mexico; Virgin Gorda, B.V.I.; Nice, France; Stanley, Idaho).

While I similarly ranged afield in:

- age (18–70);
- marital status (single–divorced);
- paternal duties (ministering to any number of kids, ranging in age from three to 23), many of whom include child characters from TV such as "Ernie" (*My Three Sons*) or "Rudy" from the *Cosby Show;*
- residences (first apartment in a Brooklyn basement; a colonial-style suburban home, presumably like the one she now lived in; a bayside manse in Tiburon, overlooking San Francisco [site of our first post-graduate, real-world vacation]; an army outpost in Antarctica, a place I'd never visited [in which she was a colonel and I was a major . . . and I didn't know which rank was higher]).

"It's nice to know that a financially strapped guy like you can afford to visit such interesting places," Beth says, "if only in your dreams. But, c'mon, you've given this reunion a great deal of conscious thought, too. What do you realistically envision will happen on Friday night?"

Realistically?

Probably something similar to what transpired during our last in-depth, face-to-face discussion, which occurred on a New Year's Eve, about 20 years ago.

Things We Said Today

Sarah and I had backed ourselves into a corner in a friend's apartment, curiously eager to discuss the turns our lives had taken in the few years since we'd finally separated. The tenor of the talk was wistful. We stood there, drinks in hand, for more than an hour.

I wondered aloud: What if we'd stayed together?

"We probably would have been divorced," Sarah said. "You forget how much we fought. We could rarely go several days without some major argument."

Or you poppin' someone else, I said.

"Whatever," she said.

She then launched into an altogether too-detailed description of some of the "communication" problems she'd been having with her husband. I tried to look as sympathetic as possible without actually listening to what she was saying (what was it my business?) . . . and nearly missed her offhanded comment: "I don't think anyone will ever know and understand me as well as you do."

The statement didn't surprise me—my perspicacity and acuity when it came to her moods and motivation were probably my major selling points—but I was surprised that she'd express it to me. To what end? Was there something I could do with this information on a night like

that—historically one of the loneliest on the calendar—
other than perhaps torture myself a little more about the
choices I'd made.

At the time, the most telling reply I could muster was
the same one she'd tossed off a few minutes earlier, the
non-response you usually use when there's so much to
say but no great motivation to collect your thoughts and
say them.

Whatever, I said.

Funny How Time Slips Away

It's funny, I say to Beth.

"Funny peculiar or humorous funny?"

Funny ironic.

"I'm listening."

When I think about Sarah, I consider myself the injured
party. I am the one she hurt again and again, and whom she
abandoned again and again. And, when she finally proposed a
lasting peace (and I could not accept), she didn't give me
enough time to heal my wounds.

"How much time would you have needed?"

I don't know. A few more months, maybe a few more years.

"Or conceivably *many* more years. Maybe never?"

Maybe.

"Schmuck."

Oy. You, too?

"If only you had listened to me 13 years ago, you might've

gotten beyond all this crap while you were young enough to do something about it."

Fuck you.

"Anytime."

Sarah may have been (thus far) the truest love, but she was far from my first.

Puppy Love

Her name was Maisie Most (it's too good a moniker to make up—I can only hope she hasn't grown into a humorless, litigious crone).

> **MAISIE**, 5, 3'6", 47 lbs.; naturally blond hair; green eyes; kindergarten student; after I met her in the playground sandbox, she remained the unrequited object of my affections until junior high school (and, as a result, taught me the requisite virtues of patience and persistence when it came to courting women).

When I threw my first fistful of sand in her direction during recess, she laughed it—and me—off. Each subsequent grade, we continued to share a classroom and the age-appropriate boy-on-girl mating rituals—hair pulling; arm pulling; rock throwing; shoving; pushing; taunting; teasing; bra snapping—as well as the annual exchange of Valentine's Day cards. In a more Darwinian era, before an all-inclusive, ultra-sanitized, gender-blind, parent-controlled childhood became the norm, kids could make, express, and distribute individualized expressions of their affection.

I was convinced that my fifth-grade effort would at last put me over the top with Maisie. Knowing that she had a crush on Richard Chamberlain—who played the title character on the popular weekly TV drama, *Dr. Kildare*—I wrote to the network and received his autographed photograph. I put the stock shot in with my homemade Valentine, on which I scrawled the straightforward (albeit, in retrospect, homoerotic) plea to "Be *Our* Valentine."

"O-o-o-h, I just lo-o-o-ve him!" she cooed when espying the fake, fey intern as I waited bootlessly for her to add: "I love you, too. But all she said was: "Thank you for the gift. That was sweet."

It would take another two years for Cupid to reveal his master plan: After a male classmate took ill with mononucleosis (ironically, it was then called "the kissing disease"), I received a last-minute invite to the seventh-grade cool kids' make-out party. There, in Rocco Frangia-something's basement, nearly eight years since I first fell for her, I found myself nose to nose, lip to lip, *tongue to tongue*, with the fair Maisie. Fortunately my orthodontic braces had been removed a week before.

"And?" Beth asks, eager to hear the outcome. "What happened!? How come I'd never heard about this little infatuation before?"

Nothing much happened. We kissed. It was okay.

"Just okay?"

Yeah.

"Typical."

What do you mean?

"Like most men, you only want what you can't have."

Was it my imagination, or was Beth becoming as sarcastic and pissy as some of my other Boys?

Beth might be right about wanting what you can't have. But she's wrong in assuming it is mostly a male thing.

"Well, you may have a point there," she says, "and I've probably been guilty of feeling—and acting—that way in my life as well. Maybe it's just a human thing: You want something or someone so badly that you even begin to convince yourself that you have *it* (whatever or whomever it is that you want) . . . but the reality cannot ever be as good as, or close to, what you imagined."

That's all I'm saying.

I'm Not Feeling It Anymore

There was Maisie—the girl of my pre-pubescent (that had become pubescent) fantasies—right in my kisser. When our lips finally locked and tongues tentatively touched, the reality was pretty damned cool . . . and way hot. But it just wasn't quite as unbelievably life-changing as I'd imagined. It was somewhat mechanical and uncomfortable, though the latter wasn't her fault. (Only the host and his girl got to make out on a couch, while the other couples had to make do with one metal bridge chair apiece.)

There was something else that seemed to spoil the

moment, but nothing that I could categorically pinpoint. Maybe it was her perfume, which was a little too robust for my olfactory sensibilities (it's almost impossible to hold your breath and kiss at the same time). Maybe it was the too-frilly embroidery deployed across the chest of her mohair pullover (mitigating any significant sweater petting). Maybe it was the way she bared her teeth and rubbed her gums against mine in the mistaken belief that it was a turn-on. (Maybe, even at 12, I was a cranky, critical sonofabitch.)

Maybe, more likely, I just didn't know her at all. She was this perfect creation of my making, and I never bothered, or couldn't get close enough, to discover the real girl behind the false front.

Writers say of editors: They don't know what they want, only what they *don't* want. The pursuit of love can be similarly described. It follows a trail of trial and error, propelling you nearer to the heart of the matter as you go.

Broken Valentine

Beth?

"I was just thinking about the Valentine's Days of my youth: the vulnerability, the waiting, and the expectations," she says. "I wouldn't want to relive those days again."

I'm sorry I brought it up. I didn't realize that Valentine's Day is such an emotionally fraught holiday.

"It's a girl thing," she says.

We decide to call it a night. Beth, a fellow sentimentalist, seems to choke up a little when she hugs and kisses me good-bye. But she's just goofing on me.

"I'm sending you out there a boy," Beth says. "But you'll be coming back a man."

I reach over and pat her ass, just for old time's sake.

"Well, maybe a teenager," she says.

5

Ain't Nothing Like the Real Thing

Friday, 6:23 PM

I stand, wait, and watch Sarah walk through the restaurant to our table.

This Is It

We don't hug, but I do kiss her airily near the cheek. (I'm not sure if I miss, or she flinches.) Evidently we are both a little anxious—no surprise, considering the great distance we've traveled in separate directions to arrive at this moment—but there is surprisingly little parrying, ducking, and dicking around (all of which have characterized every one of our previous reconciliatory reunions). But, with the issue of actual reconciliation off the table, we seem—conversationally, at least—completely unstrained and open from the get-go.

An exchange of pleasantries takes all of six minutes.

6:25–6:31 PM

"I got a cab right away," she says, "but there was a lot of traffic coming downtown."

Yeah, I forgot, I say. It's still rush hour.

The waiter appears.

"I'll have a glass of red wine, please," she says.

"Merlot?"

"Fine."

"And you, Sir?"

I look at my empty martini glass. I've been here for less than 20 minutes, and I've already consumed several ounces of pure alcohol. Better slow down a bit.

Sure, I'll have another, I say to the waiter.

Sarah reaches across the table to tug at my hair.

Ouch!

"I just wanted to see if it was real."

With that, all small talk concludes, and a candid and free-wheeling exchange of ideas, thoughts, and feelings commences.

Holding Back the Years

6:32 PM

I look her up and down and as far around as I could manage from across the table in a relatively dark room: same height; roughly the same weight, give or take; same dark eyes and hair color (though she later tells me it'd be gray if she didn't dye it); and same sienna skin and Mediterranean features (her mother is of Egyptian heritage) that so attracted me, and whose essential looks and body type I have replicated in subsequent girlfriends. (Only her once-ample bosom seems diminished with age.)

She still looks pretty good. Pretty *and* damned good for her age. Sure, a tad pinched above the lips, and the slight makings of a jowl or two, but the skin around her eyes is nearly unlined.

Did you have any work done? I ask. The top half of your face looks great.

She laughs. "No, no work . . . yet," she says. "But thanks for the compliment."

Direct, not defensive, doesn't easily take offense—I am reminded why I liked her.

Some individuals would've responded to my quasi-tactless comment with a defensive: "Why? What's wrong with the *bottom* half of my face?"

Just a few weeks ago, I accidentally ran into Francine, an ex of more recent vintage. Ever the joshing gent, I said: You look good for your age. She did not appreciate the tone, spirit, or content of my remark.

"What do you mean—*my* age?" she said in all seriousness, then frowned *accordionly*. (Maybe if she wasn't so free with those facial movements, she'd look a lot younger and better. What do you think causes those creases and crow's feet? All that pursing, flaring, and glaring.) I'd forgotten how hypersensitive and over-reactive she could be in response to the most innocuous comments.

No-no, I meant that you looked—you *look*—good . . . for any age, I said, each phumphering word making me more resentful. I wanted to grab her (gently) by each shoulder and say (not too loudly): Hey, it's just a lame joke. Lighten up!

And right there, in what should have been a pleasant three-minute encounter between two old lovers, we revisited and reaffirmed why we were *not* made for each other.

FRANCINE, 46, 5'6", weight unknown; curly black-brown hair; brown eyes; self-employed marketing consultant; said she knew I was "the one" during our first phone conversation. (She was so nervous before our first date that she threw up.) She soon decided that she wanted us to live together and get married; but, after three years, she was forced to let go of that dream when I kept finding excuses to cancel apartment-hunting appointments. Since the two of us reside in the same neighborhood, we occasionally run into each other. The first few times, her stomach would drop. More recently, she says to friends, "it's just unpleasant." Though she has had several long-term relationships since *us*, she remains unmarried.

You Really Got Me

Sarah, from what I remember, was a lot less moody, tetchy, and high-strung than Francine or, say, me. She was for the most part able to conceal her truest emotions behind a well-defended façade of wisecracks and snappy repartee. Just like most guys.

Best of all, she gave me lots of latitude to express anger or vent frustration because she was, or seemed to be, secure enough not to take it personally. She also had no problem with directness—receiving or sending. So when I stepped over the line—spraying her with misguided f-bombs, for example, or carelessly wreaking collateral damage in her vicinity—she took appropriate action.

Her prime tactic was to point out my own obvious *ridiculousness*, which could be tweaked into submission by merely holding a mirror up to it. This strategy was most effective when deployed with some humor.

To wit: A mutant (neither Mom nor Dad had it) ultra-competitive gene often tipped the balance of my equilibrium. But, instead of backing off or away from it, she took me on: in backgammon, checkers, chess, spades, poker, or the board game *Risk* (there is a priceless photo of us going *mano a mana*, staring coldly at the photographer for daring to disrupt our pursuit of world domination).

To make our matches "more interesting," we'd usually wager dinner, a concert, or sexual services. I usually won. But if and when she beat me—usually on, say, a last lucky roll, move, or pull—I became a very ill-tempered loser. My visceral response to defeat was so great that, in an insane fury (very temporary, mind you), I'd bark out wild curses and throw a fit—literally—by tossing cards, boards, or dice across the room.

After such an inexcusable display, she did not respond immediately. Instead, allowing my steam to slowly escape, she took her sweet time to—say, if we were playing backgammon—get up and stroll over to where the dice had rattled to rest. She would make a big show of staring down at them; then she'd look up and, in a bright, chirpy voice, say: "Nice roll." I couldn't help but smile. Tension deflated. Fight averted. Surrender secured.

She knew how to play me, and I didn't mind a bit.

A Lover's Question

Anticipating that, after such a lengthy dry spell, our social intercourse might need some artificial lubrication in addition to alcohol, I devise a written quiz for her to take: six questions, fill in the blanks. (This exercise also offers a smooth segue to disclose my new part-time gig—adjunct professor of freshman English—at a local city college.)

The test assesses her memory and knowledge of a half-dozen subjects:

1. **GEO-POLITICS:** Your first anti-war march as a collegian was held in   _____.

2. **ZOOLOGY:** Your father often referred to Mr. Schreiber as the   _____.

3. **BIOLOGY:** You lost your virginity in the month of   _____.

4. **NOMENCLATURE:** The name of our first boy was to be   _____.

5. **SOCIOLOGY:** The blond girl on the central committee was named   _____.

6. **LITERATURE:** Don Quixote's sidekick was named _____.

Correct responses are listed in UPPERCASE type below; her responses are *italicized.*

1.	POUGHKEEPSIE	*Albany*
2.	WOLFMAN	*Apeman*
3.	DECEMBER	*January*
4.	BRUNO MAXIMILLIAN	*Scooter*
5.	PEARL	*Pearl*
6.	SANCHO PANZA	*Ricky Ricardo*

She takes the exam in the jokey, mildly competitive spirit in which it is offered, does her best, and gets one correct answer.

When Love Was New

"You had a crush on Pearl, didn't you?" she says. "From what I recall, it could have just as easily been her sitting here tonight."

Not really. During college, she had no interest in me at all. Though—funny story—I did end up dating her for a few months.

"Do tell."

I met her at a party about a year after we broke up. She'd let herself go a bit: She had gained five, maybe 45, pounds; had just come out of rehab (for cocaine and alcohol abuse); and had started a close personal relationship with Jesus Christ (which, for some reason, meant forswearing a personal hygiene and grooming regimen, but not pre-marital sex). I couldn't resist. This was, after all, Pearl—the most beautiful girl on campus.

"Ahem," Sarah says.

Ah, yes, the *second* most beautiful girl on campus.

Numero Uno, of course, is sitting across from me, demurely sipping her red wine. I smile at the memory.

"What?" she asks.

The Most Beautiful Girl in the World

We had been going out about a week, and we couldn't keep our hands off of each other. There were, however, limits to other body parts. She was, after all, a virgin.

On our eighth night, there were the usual long, slow, deep, moan-clogged kisses and all sorts of over-the-clothing fondling, kneading, and grinding. Then she gave me the nod (as in: You may go ahead and touch my beautiful breasts).

Actually, if I remember accurately, it was her hand that gently guided mine to the back of her sweater, under and up to the hooked clasp, where it left me to complete the undoing. While I struggled briefly, she cagily smiled, as in: "Pal, you are in for one peak [pun intended] experience."

Eventually I undid and unscrolled her bra, helped her wriggle free of all cover and cloth, and then gasped—the first and only time I can ever recall gasping at the sight of anything so . . . majestic. ("Breasts" somehow seemed an inadequate description, "bosoms" anachronistic, "tits" a sacrilege.)

It may have been in that moment, having glimpsed on earth a vision so exquisite and ineffable, that I first seriously considered the delicate hand of God. Only a Divine Being could conceive and construct such perfect form.

Jeez, Lord, You do some good work . . .

(I'd be ungallant if I revealed too much about our sex life together, but I'd be even more unjust to you, the reader, if I didn't disclose at least a few pertinent, prurient details about our first time.)

Like a Virgin

We were in no rush. We'd talked about it; we knew it was only a matter of time. We were both a little nervous:

She had never done *it*, and I had barely more experience, though how much more was indeterminate. (I was pretty sure that I had fulfilled penetration and climax—I just didn't remember if they occurred at the same time, and with whom.)

Finally, in December, we were both ready.

"I still think it was January," Sarah says. "I'm pretty sure we waited *three* months."

No, I say, you just like to think that you weren't so easy. It was definitely before New Year's. In fact, I think it was right before Christmas vacation. And, if I recall, we did it in Jay Franklin's room; he'd already gone home for the holidays.

"That sounds so romantic," she says. "We '*did it*' in his room."

Well, we did. And I even remember the room number: 307.

"You're sure it wasn't 309?" she says. "A woman never forgets her first."

Nor does a man.

God Only Knows

After we'd made love for the first time, my body lay there in complete satisfaction, while my exploding, still-evolving teenaged brain began to question the heavens: "Why me? What had I done to deserve such karmic largesse? Was there a bargain struck without my knowledge for which I would somehow be made to pay for years to come?" (Apparently, yes.)

Why me, indeed. I was not especially handsome, not in the way that she was traffic-stoppingly striking. Nor would it would not have been inaccurate to call me pasty-faced, even in the dead of summer. At best, as evinced by my freshman ID card, I was cute. That photo, however, was taken weeks before the appearance of—in retrospect—one of the most ridiculously configured, completely half-assed, jawline-rimming beards ever witnessed outside of Amish Country, the White House (1861–1865), or the home of basketball player/announcer Bill Walton (mid to late 1970s).

I couldn't speak for the Amish people, or for Abraham Lincoln, but I could probably intuit what would compel left-leaning hoopsters such as Mr. Walton and myself to brave such silly, woolly whiskers. (Because: we *could*.)

It wasn't much. It wasn't pretty. It didn't even have an accompanying mustache. But, most importantly, my girlfriend liked and encouraged it.

Friday, 7:46 PM

Sarah and I continue to argue like an old married couple—though with none of the bile and edge—about the number of times we'd broken up.

"Six," she says.

I think it was seven.

"Maybe eight," she says.

We finally agree that we broke up more times than either of us could count.

For me, without a doubt, the first time was by far the worst. That was true heartbreak. I thought then that I'd never get over it, and I probably never did.

The Birth of the Blues

During our freshman school year, Sarah and I made plans to travel cross-country during summer vacation, but my parents put their kibosh on that plan by saying that I had to stay home and earn some money. And so I worked at a succession of real jobs—cutting and packing in a glass factory; pumping, wiping, and dip-sticking at a gas station; driving, delivering, stocking, and vacuuming at the local pharmacy; and, finally, picking up garbage with a sharp stick on several state highways—while Sarah's folks funded an eight-week archaeological dig in Israel.

She boarded the plane in tears, vowing her undying love for me. However, each successive letter of hers arrived with less frequency and ardor:

- "I love you as much as the whole wide world."
- "I love you a bushel and a peck."
- "I love you."
- "With love."

And then at the near-end of summer, after not hearing a word from her for two weeks, my most dire and insecurity-laden fears (which I made the mistake of expressing and mailing) were affirmed:

"Yes, it's true, I've been seeing someone else . . . "

"You're not going to pull out my old letters, are you?" she asks.

No, but I still have them.

"Excuse me," the waiter interrupts. "Would you like to hear the specials?"

If you don't mind, I say, I need a little more time to stew in my self-pity. (What I actually say is more like: Undying love was supposed to last a lot longer than a year.)

"Certainly, Sir," the waiter says. "Take as much time as you need."

It's a Hard-Knock Life

Her leave-taking was incomprehensible to me. The chosen one had chosen someone else. Joseph Conrad, Stephen King, and Barbara Cartland could not have adequately described the horror, the misery, or the heartbreak.

The unbreakable bond was broken. My baby done gone, and woe, O Lord, was me. All was lost. I was like a buoy adrift, no help on the horizon. (In every man, there's still a little buoy.)

I woke up every day to a feeling that can only be described as "blue." The deep, deep blues. (That's when I became a fervent devotee to *the* blues, and to all sad and beautiful music, which could take you to places so desolate and empty that you'd have no alternative but to feel better.) It was a sadness so profound that I had no doubt it would last all my days. (It didn't, but the love of this music did.)

According to the oft-quoted Nietzsche slogan: "That which does not kill us makes us stronger." And, as Hemingway similarly proffered: "The world breaks everyone and afterward many are strong at the broken places."

I might have been broken, but I was still breathing. Ergo: I was stronger.

Brand New Me

Well, I *appeared* to be. To salvage my shattered self-esteem, and protect myself from any further—and future—anguish, I began to construct an ostensibly tougher, crustier, Hemingway-esque persona. As such, I acted out in all sorts of pseudo-macho, marginally self-destructive ways: punching out dorm windows; jumping out of two-story buildings; screwing—or *trying* to screw—every co-ed in sight . . .

I built a persona right out of the tough guy's handbook: hard, inscrutable, implacable . . . a man's man . . . a poker player who played it close to the vest and never gave an inch . . . and a lone wolf who relied on his wits, never depending on anyone but himself . . .

"From what I heard, you were flat-out nuts," Sarah says.

Oh, that's right, you had to hear everything second-hand. And why was that?

"Because you refused to speak to me," she says. "You refused to even acknowledge me. If you saw me on campus, you would walk past me as if I'd ceased to exist."

A brilliant plan, I might add, that fooled *you*. One night, I remember—right after I finished playing you some new musical discovery (I think it was Fred Neil or Joni Mitchell)—you said to me, "For a tough guy, how come you like such maudlin songs?" In fact, it was a line from Joni Mitchell's *Blue* album ("The Last Time I Saw Richard") that made you think of it: *You got tombs in your eyes, but the songs you punched are dreaming . . .*

"You're not still nuts, are you?" she says.

Every Day I Write the Book

I've seriously thought about writing one of those little gift books, maybe calling it *Break Up 2 Make Up: Tips for Young Guys to Win Back Their Lost Love(s)*. Perfect for Valentine's Day.

"And what sort of material would this booklet include?" she asks.

Mainly self-help tips. A few how-to suggestions. And, to give it a narrative flow, a bunch of stories—cautionary tales, amusing anecdotes, and hard-won lessons—taken mostly from my life, but also mixed in with other folks' experiences.

"Could you share some sample material with me?"

Sure.

Every Time You Go Away

The following is excerpted from the proposed *Break Up 2 Make Up: Tips for Young Guys to Win Back Their Lost Love(s)*. All Rights Reserved.

I met Kalipinya [not her real name] a month into my freshman year of college. The following summer, she left me for an older, richer, handsomer guy she'd met during a tour of Europe. Sure, I was devastated at the breakup, but I did not show it, certainly never to her.

TIP #1: KEEP IT TO YOURSELF

By concealing your pain, she might even wonder if you ever cared that much about her to begin with, which might make you more appealing (and definitely more appealing than if you'd begged or pleaded for her not to leave you).

Incandescent Gesture

While Kalipinya was away, I'd bought her a bicycle for her birthday, which we'd planned to celebrate at summer's end. Though logistically problematic—she lived an hour away, plus we weren't speaking [see below]—I decided to give it to her anyway. This meant waking at 4 AM (I needed to return my father's car before he left for work at 7:30); picking up my buddy Strauss; driving to Kalipinya's home; hopping the four-foot-high metal backyard fence; lifting the bike over the fence; setting it down on its kickstand without damage; hopping back over and getting away without being seen; arriving back home by 7. We did it; so can you.

TIP #2: ALWAYS DEPART ON A HIGH NOTE

She's already gone, and there's nothing you can do . . . for now. But you can ensure that the last thing she remembers is your classy gesture. If it engenders an iota of guilt, you've done your job.

Hymns to the Silence

After the grand gesture leaves her reeling—well, perhaps, not reeling, but not as dead-sure of her decision as she was when she made it—you want her to want something more from you (even if it's nothing more than a chance for her to say, "thank you"). But she won't receive that opportunity, nor anything else from you. After our breakup, I often ran into my ex around campus. The first couple of times, she smiled nervously when she spotted me and was about to say something when I brushed past her with nary a word or a second glance. (I'm sure that, had I turned around to look, her mouth would've been left hanging and there'd be surprise—and maybe even curiosity—in her eyes.) At that point, silence was the only avenue of rebuff open to me, and I never failed to take it.

TIP #3: LEAVE HER AGAPE IN YOUR WAKE

By refusing to acknowledge her presence, or even existence, you might make her start her thinking about you. Maybe not immediately, but in due time, which is your biggest ally (as well as your greatest enemy). If nothing else, you will begin to reclaim the one prize that no one can keep: your self-esteem.

Building a Mystery

With luck, your silence has created curiosity, wonder, and interest—all potential benefits in your long-term plan to win her back. Now's the time to construct and sustain a little buzz, or hype, about yourself. Since you're not speaking to her, you'll have to leave it to others to carry your message. It's Public Relations 101: manipulation of the messengers (your mutual friends). How? By creating a myth. By doing and saying things so outrageous and daring that she'll have to hear about some of them. And, even if she only finds out about one-half of your escapades, the stories will soon take on lives of their own . . . as your messengers begin to embellish and elaborate on the truth; in effect, massaging your message into mysteriously mythical proportions. And who can resist a good mystery or myth? Not her.

> ## TIP #4: WHEN IT COMES TO WINNING HEARTS
> ## AND MINDS IN THE DATING WARS,
> ## PERCEPTION IS HALF THE BATTLE

"Not something I'd buy my husband for Valentine's Day." she says. "But hopefully there's a market for this kind of material."

That's what I'm hoping, too.

Who Knows Where the Time Goes?

"By the way, have you been back to see the old campus?" Sarah asks. "I took my kids a few years ago. It looks about the same."

A friend of mine has a country house nearby, I say, but I've only been on the school grounds twice. The first time, maybe six or eight years after you and I graduated, was a nice nostalgic visit. I remember being pleasantly surprised to see the names of our intramural teams inscribed on the various championship trophies: Meatball Heroes for softball; Red Ralphs for volleyball; Scungil Wizards for basketball.

Maybe five years ago, I was jazzed to take three contemporary pals on a personal tour down such abundantly fertile memory lanes. It turned out to be a complete downer. (*Jazzed? Downer?* Never quite a hippie, too young for a beatnik . . . but, apparently, that doesn't stop me from occasionally sounding like one.) The old trophies had run out of scribing room, and were scrapped for newer Heroes and Wizards—not one of our athletic achievements remained in sight. Even more traumatic was the proliferation of old ghosts.

As we four coots walked through one of the classroom buildings, we were swept along with the students. For me, the sensation of being an underclassman prowling these halls became so familiar, so immediate, that it went beyond nostalgia. I was *living* it.

I had no capacity to detach myself from the original experience. I was there. I became lost in time, straddling two planes in the same world: one foot in *then*, the other foot in *now*. And I didn't know where to step next.

When I snapped out of it, I was overcome with such emotion that I had to go sit in the can until I could regather myself.

"What was it that so upset you?" Sarah asks.

I was standing in the same spot that I'd once asked myself: Where would the years take me? Then I was there, and it seemed like I hadn't moved a muscle since then.

Where *did* the years go? I could only hope that they were being stored somewhere, waiting for the right time and place in which they could be exhibited for more than a few passing memories.

"You really are one sentimental sap," she says, not unkindly.

I don't say it to her, but I was also reminded of the palpable sorrow that squeezed my stomach while I slunk through those halls during our many "breaks."

Do It Again

Our first breakup lasted from August 'till April—virtually an entire school year of silence and myth-making—with a makeup that fortuitously bloomed right before finals.

And we repeated this breakup-makeup pattern for a total of six years, off and on.

Do It Again

And . . .

Do It Again

And . . .

Do It Again

And . . .

Do It Again

Until it was (had we not kept breaking up) our fourth consecutive summer. We had both graduated from college. Things were getting serious; we even started to talk (joke?) about marriage, for which we both agreed on one essential criterion: a total of $2,000 in the bank.

Once again, on her parents' dime, she went off to Israel—this time to work on a kibbutz—and I stayed behind to begin my life's work (and receive decreasingly demonstrative airmails).

Everything Old Is New Again

"What made you keep coming back for more?" she asks.

Good question. Why did I allow her to continually break my heart and spirit? Why did I persistently pursue the pain, the passion and (oh, what the hell) the *pussy* rather than tend to unhealed scars; reflect on a loftier purpose; or find someone who did not *seem* quite as perfect but was far more loyal?

Why indeed?

- Because *Love Has No Pride.*
- Because I was weak in *Body and Soul.*
- Because I got weak at the thought of *her* body.
- Because I was young and ruled by my johnson.
- Because I thought we had a connection so strong and celestial that it could not be tainted or weakened by the venial sins of mortal man or woman.
- Because I believed that there was nothing better than "beginnings"—when something was new and fresh and rife with possibility—and . . .
- Because, by continually breaking up and making up, we could keep it relatively new and fresh each time.

What was *your* excuse? I ask her. Why did you keep coming back?

"I remembered that you were my soul mate," she says.

Okay. And, as long as we're talking about it: Why did you keep breaking up with me?

"My own tremendous insecurities," she says.

Really? That surprised me a little. What caused them?

"Many factors. D.N.A. My father's critical nature. The fact that I developed at an early age, and men began chasing after me primarily for my physical attributes."

Okay, that sounds reasonable.

"Oh, and probably most important," she adds, "is that I found it difficult to be so emotionally attached to someone. Being so vulnerable and exposed made it impossible to hide from you . . . and myself as well. Maybe, for some people, that's fine. But, for me, it might be too much to sustain in a relationship. Even today. Being somewhat emotionally distanced from Bill at times has enabled me to have—at least the perception—of privacy, which is something I feel that I need. I certainly did back then."

Now *that* sounded true and right—for both of us.

Blame It on My Youth

Could you forgive a woman—even if she was only a girl at the time—for causing so much pain?

To be equally true and fair, it was often my own insecurity that made me so quick to respond to and dissect her frequent flights of fancy (possibility inducing actual flight) when most often the best course of action would have been to let it, and her, be.

On a middling day, I had some difficulty comprehending what a beautiful, interesting girl like her saw in me. In my darkest hours, I questioned how, and if, I'd be able to sustain her interest. The rest of the time, I stayed attuned to her moods and, when I perceived a shift in attentiveness or affection on her part, tried to recalibrate or reverse the downward spiraling process. Basically I tried to *control* it, and her.

There were two major flaws in my thinking process:

- she would instinctively and emphatically rebel against any effort on my part to control her;
- since she did believe that I knew her so well, she took as gospel my suspicions and suppositions.

"If you thought my attentions were wandering," she confirms, "then I assumed they were."

My beliefs and behavior would come as a shock to every subsequent girlfriend, most of whom railed at me time and again for my withholding, detached nature. Caring too little was what they believed of me. Caring too much would seem to them unthinkable.

I remade myself for that very reason: so I would never again care as much; so I would never again experience such anguish; so I would never again be in thrall to forces outside of my control.

Acknowledging these sentiments precipitated a question—for myself: Would I under any circumstances take her back *now*?

6

The Kind of Love You Never Recover From

Friday, 8:34 PM

It has been an enriching and enlightening couple of hours. I continue to be amazed at how easily and freely we interact— no muss or fuss, no struggle or restraint, no censoring of feelings (and little thought as to how they might play at home). The evening has exceeded my own, and anyone else's, expressed expectations.

Dinner—the main course—is nearly done. As are our two drinks. Our conversational fare, however, soon takes a magnum leap forward.

Daddy's Girl

"My father passed away seven years ago," she says, her eyes glistening.

I didn't know, I say. I'm so sorry. I am tempted to place a comforting hand on hers.

"He went in for a simple procedure," she says, "but never made it out."

He was some piece of work, her father—a tough, old bird (though, when I met him, probably not much older than I currently am), cue bald, who looked like that scowling cartoon eagle whose name I can't place, as well as the British actor Donald Pleasence. He had few overtly kind words for anyone except, on occasion, his daughter. He referred to me as "the wolfman" (though not to my hairy face), a relatively apt comment on the reddish, continuish sideburns that ran from one side of my face to the other. The thing is: I liked her dad, probably 'cause I sensed that beneath our respective gruff/scruff exteriors was some kindred spirit. Which is what probably attracted her to me in the first place. That and the thought of pissing him off.

"When he died," Sarah says, "I didn't take it very well."

Who does.

"I had to be strong for my mother. But, when I got home, no one was there for me. Not my kids—who were, after all, just kids . . ."

I know what you mean.

"And not my husband, who was also of little comfort. Maybe it's because he was never close to his own parents. Whatever the reason, there was just a huge emotional disconnect."

Hmmm.

"And that's when I thought of calling you."

Yeah, well . . . (I am listening to her, but I might have drifted back for a sec . . . probably to the bottomless grief of my own dad's passing. Not a day has gone by without me thinking of him. Many mornings, in fact, begin with the unsettling, late-dawning realization of his absence. After all, I'd just seen him in my dreams . . .)

Wha-a-a-a-t—?!

And then her words float out to me, like a distant phone, b-b-b-r-r-r-ing-g-g-ing me back to consciousness. I struggle back to the surface, swimming through the water in my own eyes.

Excuse me, *what did you just say?*

Real Real Gone

"I thought about contacting you seven years ago when my father died," she says. "Bill just didn't, or couldn't, get it. I needed much more emotionally from him. And I knew that you could give that to me. So I thought seriously about calling you."

But?

"But, in the end, I decided that it would've been too unfair . . ."

To whom?

"To you, my husband . . . I don't know."

If this were another time, or place, I likely would have gotten up from the table and gone over to give her a hug. But I keep seated, and I keep my hands to myself; even a soothing pat seems too shallow and minimal a gesture.

I nod gravely, while traveling back in brain time. Seven years ago? I try to recollect what I was working on; who I was "dating" (an outdated word, I know, for someone my age); or how I would have responded to her call.

Would I have been there for her in the way that she wanted and needed? How would I have felt about the sudden intrusion into my life? And where could it possibly have led?

"It's incredible," she continues, "how naïve you can be. You hear about friends' parents dying all the time. You try and comfort the living. You convey as much understanding and empathy as you can possibly can. Even when people close to you die—grandparents, aunts, uncles—you feel sadness, sure, and you attempt to say all the right things to their surviving mates, siblings, or children. . . . But you know what?"

Sure *I do.*

"You don't have a clue what it feels like until it hits your own home. You somehow think that 'never' or 'always' apply to you and your loved ones. How can you possibly accept that you'll *never* see or talk to your father again?"

I know. *It's all over but the shouting.*

"What?" she says.

That phrase: *It's all over but the shouting.* I know where it comes from, and what it's supposed to represent, but it makes no sense. Same thing with: *It's not over till the fat lady sings.* If the fat lady is still singing, it's not over, right? And if someone, anyone, is still shouting, then it can't quite be over. *It ain't over till it's over.* Now *that* one makes complete sense. In my opinion, Yogi Berra understood the meaning of real loss.

My thoughts are admittedly wandering a bit afield. But I am still processing the bombshell that she dropped just a few minutes ago . . .

I *say:* Now that I, too, am a member of that non-exclusive club of mourners, I truly and completely understand your pain.

"I knew you would," she says.

We aren't finished with our evening, not by a long shot . . . another round for both of us . . . and several other startling admissions from her. For the first time since she arrived, I look at my watch: only **9:33 PM.**

We have time.

I'll Keep It with Mine

"After my father died," she says, "my brothers and I spent a very emotional day going through his effects. In his safe, we found four letters that he'd written to his wife and three children."

What did yours say?

"He told me how proud he was of me, and how much he loved me."

Can't ask for more than that.

"When *I* die," she says, "my family will go through my things, and you know what they'll find?"

Your letters to them?

"*Your* letters and poems."

Mine as in me? I ask.

"Yeah."

It's like a real-life *Bridges of Madison County* . . .

"You know," she says, "I still have your first book."

That would be the "book" of poems and prose pieces that I stapled inside two pieces of cardboard and gave her as a 20th birthday present. (My little brother, then about 12, did the illustrations. On the front: a drawing of a convertible with two people sitting in it; on the back: same car and driver, but no passenger. I had to redo the back cover at the last minute to reflect current events: another breakup.)

"You always were a romantic fellow."

Again she's likely the only woman I ever dated who would articulate that sentence. But I did often wonder about the "book." Did she still have it? Had anyone else read it? In my darker broodings, I imagined that she had permitted her husband—or kids, too, for that matter—to have a peek. And maybe they all had a good laugh at my juvenile, romantically foolish expense.

Where do you keep it? I ask.

"It's buried deep in one of my 'personal' drawers. No one else has ever seen it."

I'm glad. Thanks. That is a relief.

"I can still quote some of my favorite lines," she says.

Uh-no. Please don't.

"*The ends of the earth are many, if any*," she quotes. "*The loves of my life are few; they is you.*"

What can I say? (What would *you* say? Cutesy? Lame? Acutely embarrassing?)

"Do you remember, *Stay?*" she asks.

Unfortunately I do.

"*Everyall I do or say/Is/Stay*," she says. (Yeah, *everyall*—one word. That was during my e.e. cummings phase.)

Man, this is painful. There are two things that I have vowed never to do as an adult: 1) allow photographs to be taken of me while *fast* dancing; 2) reread any poetry I ever wrote as a kid.

Let's talk about something else, I say.

It's All in the Game

"You know, in preparation for tonight, I *Googled* you," she says. "I saw that you'd written five real books."

Actually eight. A few are out of print.

"I was disappointed."

What do you mean?

"They're mostly about sports."

I took a big martini gulp and responded a little irritably: So? I write what they pay me to write. That's my job.

"I didn't mean to imply that I'm disappointed in you, or that you should be disappointed. I don't know anyone else who's written *one* book. It's just that I always thought it would be much more satisfying for you to write about more personal things. From what I remember, your best stuff always included your own heartfelt observations, and descriptions of the people and places that meant the most to you."

How does she know about my best stuff? She's only read what I wrote *as a boy* (and one relatively recent article that she happened to see in her local paper, *Newsday*, about my experience driving in the demolition derby).

Regardless, I have no snappy comeback. She has me dead to rights. Trapped, gutted, and deep fried. I am genuinely surprised that she has it in her. I mean, I know she has the insight; I didn't think she'd spent all that much time applying it to me. I also have to hand it to her: I could not have crafted a better segue.

I've Been Working

Funny you should mention it, I say. That's "the project" I wanted to talk to you about. (Yeah, remember *that*? It was, after all, the purported reason for this meeting.)

I tell her all about this book I've begun to outline . . . the title, the subject, the leading figures, the truth about their (our) lives . . . even some of the "sex" stuff . . .

"I had a feeling this day might come."

That sounds like a line I should know, though I am blanking on the source. It sounds clever, though, and I laugh. And, following a swallow of liquid courage, I ask the question that has actually kept me up nights: Would you have any . . . ?

Before I can finish the sentence, she says: "No."

No objections?

"None."

But you don't know what I'm going to write.

"I trust you."

What about your kids?

"My son doesn't read, and my daughter's too preoccupied with her own life."

Your husband? What about Bill?

"He can take it."

That's cold. You don't think he might be upset by some of these revelations?

"He probably will be."

And that's not a problem?

"I can live with it."

(That was a load off my mind, and no doubt a major one dropped on poor hubby. Hmmm. Sounds like some discord on the home front. Well, it isn't *my* problem.)

You don't think it's a little pathetic? I say.

"What do you mean?"

Me. Pathetic. Can't let go. Can't move on.

"No, I don't think you're pathetic. On the contrary, I think it's brave of you to come to me, after all this time, not knowing how I'd respond. And, even more so, to be willing to put it out there for everybody to read. I wish I could be as brave."

But isn't it a bit pathetic that it has taken me this long?

"You may have a point there."

All the Way

"What about *your* sex life?" she asks.

Uh, excuse me. I didn't know we were getting that personal.

"In the book," she says, "how much of your sexual history is revealed? It only seems fair. If you're going to embarrass me and my family with bawdy tales, you should at least include a few about yourself."

I was under the impression that I had.

"No, it's mostly been about my nakedness and virginity."

Well, do you have anything particular in mind?

"How about *your* first time?"

You'd think I'd remember every last detail about my first time, including at least the date, place, and precise time.

It was in the afternoon, right before or right after my 18th birthday in early June—no spring chicken, sexually speaking—when the voluptuous Flora Z. spontaneously gave me the gift of penetration.

Flora, who was in my senior-year English class, was a free-spirited, brassiere-eschewing—dare I say, hippie—chick who was not at all offended by my undisguised interest in her sheer nipples. Whenever she caught me copping a peek, she'd deepen my blush with a mischievous wink. But, prior to the moment she brazenly invited me over to her house, we'd exchanged little more than winks and nods.

I'd been beginning to think that my time would never come. My doofiest, nerdiest friends had been well over the hump for a while. Hey, I thought, what about non-doofy me?

"I think you're cute," Flora said, soon after we'd sat down on her bed.

"You, too," I said.

Flora and I not only shared a similar level of attraction and English comprehension skills, but also the exact same height (5′10″) and weight (148 pounds). In a no-doubt conscious way, she reminded me of the aptly named Mrs. Grand, the eighth-grade social studies teacher who inspired my first wet dream.

When I finally got the hint (she kept tossing restlessly around on the bed—touching my hand, brushing against my thigh, even lingering for a moment on my crotch), I leaned over and kissed her. Our clothes came off in seconds. As, unfortunately, did I. Since neither of us had a condom at hand, I withdrew before spilling my seed on her grand thighs.

Later, I told my friends that I'd finally "lost my cherry," but they demurred.

"You gotta be in there at least three minutes for it to count," said Iannello.

"It's only official if you come inside her," said Strauss.

I rejected their reasoning as totally bogus—they were both notorious chain yankers—but allowed myself the possibility that, in certain primitive cultures, I could still be considered a virgin.

Vow

"There'll be no sex tonight," Sarah says.

Uh-okay. Even though we've been discussing the subject, her comment strikes me as totally non-sequiturish.

"My husband made me promise," she adds.

No problem, I say. Sure, over the years I'd fantasized about various physical permutations (like when, during lovemaking,

I'd occasionally transpose Sarah's face and/or body), and of course I'd thought about showing her:

- a few new tricks;
- a taste of what she'd missed;
- that all previous encounters could be blamed on my ignorant youth.

But, on our first night together in twenty-odd years, my wildest fantasy includes nothing more than an emotional re-coupling. It's unthinkable that as much as a kiss on the mouth would pass between *us*: a married woman and a single man.

I am quite cognizant that she's another man's wife. (You don't have to be an ordained congregant in the marriage communion to believe in its sanctity.) It seems evident that, for both of us, a physical affair is not an option. We would not sully our perfect memories with any furtive quickies.

You Are Not Alone

There are, however, many less scrupulous forces loose in the land. At the very moment that we are affirming our chastity, millions of avowed marital congregants across the United States are breaking their sacraments with a renewed passion.

Who knew? Apparently we're not spearheading a new movement, but are just another couple of carriers in an epidemic that—according to a front-page story in the *Boston Globe*—is already a discernible trend and "growing phenomenon." Facilitated by Internet dating services like Match.com, Reunion.com, Classmates.com, lostlovers.com, and kiss.com (as differentiated from Kissonline.com or http://www.kisspsychocircus.com, two sites devoted to the decked-out, made-up rock band), millions of "long-lost sweethearts" are looking "each other up years or decades later [to] find their old love return with a passion . . . at the expense of their current marriages."

Psychologist Nancy Kalish, founder of lostlovers.com, said in the *Globe* that her fellow therapists tend to underestimate the powerful nature of old loves, especially first loves, by telling such patients their rekindled feelings are based on fantasy, and they could find the same feelings in their own marriages if they tried. Kalish dismisses any attempt to minimize the powerful and unique effects of first love: "This is not about sex, it is not about the spouse or the marriage, it is not a midlife crisis. The reunion is a continuation of a love that was interrupted."

Psychologist Linda Waud, who wrote her dissertation on three reunited couples, theorizes that a teenager may attach specifically to a first lover in much the same way as a baby attaches to a mother. "There is an actual neurological attachment that happens between these individuals," Waud says, "and that's why it's enduring and it never leaves your mind. It's there forever and ever."

While it may be disappointing to discover that I am not such a pioneer, or to learn that similarly (neurologically) attached compatriots are breaking commandments left and right, it is reassuring to realize that I am not entirely alone.

My hands may be tied (sexually, and ethically, speaking), but I am still free to ask myself another important question: If circumstances were different, would we (Sarah and I) have remained in the forefront of this movement—analyzing and assessing the ramifications for generations to come—or would we be in the backseat doing "it" now?

7

The Back Nine

Sure, I say to the waiter, we'll take a look at the dessert menu.
(Yes, somewhere during all this verbiage, we did find time to
eat dinner.)

"Another drink, Sir?" he asks.

Sure.

Sarah, too, nods affirmatively. Our *third*, but who's counting?

Still buzzed from the last heady round, we prepare to "make
the turn" (in golf parlance, to head to the 10th tee for the final
holes, or "back nine," where pressure and expectations rise
exponentially).

By my reckoning, up to that point, there've been at least three
significant—I daresay *shocking*—revelatory reports on her part:

- that she seriously considered calling me after her father
  died;

- that she had no objection to me writing about our
  relationship;

- and that she didn't overly care whether her husband
  did or not.

There is at least one more explosive shot to be detonated.

Wonderful Remark

Did you ever cheat on your husband? I ask.

"No," she says. "I've never seriously thought about sleeping with another guy. Except you."

Really? (No, that wasn't her big confession. That was fairly minor in light of the one she would soon make.)

So, if we'd gotten married, would you have been faithful to me?

"Yes." (Not that either.)

What about Bill?

"As far as I know, he's been faithful to you."

Heh, heh.

"I don't think he's ever had an affair," she continues. "But, years ago, he did contact and see an ex-girlfriend, *the* ex, and didn't tell me about it until months later."

So, is this payback?

"No," she says, then qualifies: "Well, when I first received your e-mail, that might've been part of my thinking. That and the curiosity factor. But not anymore. Not now."

Then, she turns serious and—*yep, this is it*—bears in on me with a searing look of vulnerability and defiance.

"If someone would ask me if I've had a good marriage," she says, "I would say: 'Overall, yes.'

"And if someone would ask if I love my husband, I'd also say: 'Overall, yes.'"

(Wait for it.)

"But if someone ever asked me if I married my soul mate, I'd have to answer them truthfully: 'No. That one got away.'"

Hurts So Good

That's all she wrote, folks. Thank you and good night. Drive safely.

Need I say more? (So, it's a 101-page book. We'll just make the type bigger, reduce the cover price.)

Poof—or poomph. There they go: many of my doubts and insecurities; negative thoughts I've used to fill the silence; and hours I've spent on fear and foolishness. And there it is: she says it. We *are* soul mates. We feel the same way about each other.

But what the hell good can come from that information now? Aside from the titillation for you (the reader), who benefits from that information? (Not me; not really. Certainly, not Bill. And, apparently, not her.)

"Let's change the subject," she says. "There must be some other questions that you wanted to ask me. I can think of at least one."

What's that?

"You're curious to know: what happened to my full, D-cupped breasts? And: how come I'm wearing *these* imposters?"

Well, now that you mention it, I say, laughing. (See? She is still able to play me.)

"Two words: breast feeding," she says. "Those hungry little monsters sucked 'em dry . . . literally."

Ah, there is an image to remove from the fantasy bank.

"It's life, Lee," she says. "Get over it."

She rarely ever used my name. It must be something significant she is trying to say to me. And it is, of course. The gist is this: We're not 21 years old anymore.

(Such an) Easy Question

"Can I ask you a question?" she asks.

You just did.

"Why haven't you ever gotten married?"

Ah, that. Do you want the pre-packaged-condensed-wiseass-none-of-your-fucking-business response, or the one I'm still trying to figure out?

"Both."

Hmm. It's been so long since I've answered this question honestly.

"Even to yourself?"

I guess it's not something that I choose to think about all that much.

"Then why are you here?"

Because it is time I asked and answered:

- Are you "the one" that got away?

- Did I *not* marry you for the right reasons?

- Are my remembrances of our relationship accurate, or have I been clinging to self-protective delusions?

- Is this supposed idealization of youth (and the perfect girl who accompanied it) *the* thing that has prevented me from finding happiness with someone else?

"So you do ask yourself the 'marriage' question," she says. "Several questions, in fact."

I guess I do.

"And what's the answer?"

I still don't have *one.*

I Still Haven't Found What I'm Looking For

"So?"

What?

"What's the *real* answer?"

Man, she is pushy. The theories abound, I say.

"Such as?"

I've always identified with the hero riding off into the sunset alone.

"No, *really*," she says.

Man, she is relentless.

Okay:

- *You Can't Hurry Love.*

- No amount of *Wishing or Hoping* will transform something (or someone) that (who) is not into someone/thing that/who is.

- *I Done Got Old.*

"Is that it?"

You want the *real* truth? It's my androgynous first name. I think that has probably scarred me more deeply than anything else, especially in trying to connect with the opposite sex. If I'm not sure of my own gender . . .

"Fine," she says, "if you really don't want to talk about it."

Okay, fine, I tell her. I just haven't met the right person.

"Ah." She seems a mite pained by that reply.

I don't mean it that way. I mean: I haven't met the right person when everything else has been in place.

"What kinds of things would you need in place?"

Financial security, for one.

"How's that coming?"

Great. This dinner is my first meal out in six months.

"What if you'd had a rich wife supporting you?"

Not so easy to find. There have been some women who intimated that my income, or lack thereof, would not be an insurmountable obstacle to marriage . . .

"But?"

But I guess they weren't the right ones. Or they didn't seem to be at the time.

"Do you have an ego problem about being supported financially?"

Not really, considering that virtually every woman I've dated in the last 25 years has made more money than me. Although . . .

"Yes?"

In retrospect, there were two or three women I probably should've given more of a legitimate shot.

"Who were they? When? Where? What happened?"

Connie, Suzy, Patricia-Jane.

"That's four women," she said.

No, Patricia-Jane is one person. And they were all relatively recent. I met P-J at a bachelor auction. She couldn't afford to "buy" me, but we exchanged numbers and dated for a few months.

"What did you do to her?"

It was more what I did *not* do. She was 26 and had just moved back in with her parents while studying for her doctorate in psychology. And I made a big thing about being too old—I was 42—to go out and schmooze with parents every time I picked up a girl for a date. For a while, she patiently drove into the city to see me, but soon decided that my lack of effort indicated a paucity of overall commitment. After she broke up with me, I realized how much I did—or could—care about her, and I tried to change her mind. But this was a no-nonsense woman who knew what she wanted, and did not want to deal with a supposed grown man's nonsense. I often think about her.

"And then?" Sarah asks.

Connie. Right after Patricia-Jane. Again, there were some "age" issues. Connie was 14 years younger, and I think the gap bothered me.

"Bothered *you*?" Sarah says. "You don't often hear older men say that."

It was probably just a convenient excuse. I blamed most of our problems on her immaturity and neediness, not to mention her ignorance about historical events (many of which I'd lived through) and musical artists. But that was just a lame justification for *my* immaturity, neediness, and ignorance.

"Same thing with Suzy?" she asks.

No, not really. We only had one date, but I thought it was an excellent one. She was—is—a magazine writer of some note, and we really seemed to hit it off. But she blew me off when I called to ask her out again. About a year later—by then, married with baby fever—she called to apologize.

"That's all—just to apologize?"

Yeah, it was as if she'd joined a 12-step program for addictive daters, and was reaching out to all of the prospective boyfriends she had led on. She just wanted to say that, in fact, there was some chemistry between us, and if she hadn't gone back to her on-and-off-again beau, now her husband, we might've had something special. I found it strange, but also endearing.

"How old was she?"

Maybe five or six years younger than me.

"I always meant to ask you," Sarah says. "Whatever happened with Grace?"

I don't know. We fought too much, I guess.

"It seemed that you had a real connection with her."

We did. We do. I especially liked the way we made up.

"That sounds familiar."

You know, I say, this is starting to feel kind of pathetic—going through my list of women with you. It reminds me of the Jack Nicholson character in *Carnal Knowledge* (you young people really should rent this 1971 movie), who at the end—after screwing up every relationship for one reason or another—sits alone with his scrapbook of old girlfriends.

"If I recall," Sarah says, "he wasn't alone; he was with a hooker, played by Rita Moreno."

See? I say. That's something a much younger woman would not know.

"What about kids?" Sarah asks.

You think I should date *children*?!

"Not funny," she says. "Don't you want kids of your own? You seem to be such an attentive, loving uncle. And I remember how good you were with my nephews years ago."

Unk in [a] Funk

I love kids, I say. We speak the same language. I don't patronize them. I still feel connected—maybe a little too connected—to the child in me. And my nephews and nieces—those four angels/devils who share a bloodline—have had a profound effect on me. I can't imagine loving any kids more. When they leave, after spending a weekend with me, I miss them terribly. But, because I'm constantly available and open with them, it's too exhausting (especially at my age). I don't think I could sustain that complete level of emotional connectedness on a daily basis.

"You'd soon find that, as a parent, you can't always be available and open."

Recently I have thought about what it might be like to be a father, much more than I've seriously contemplated becoming a husband.

"Don't they usually go hand in hand?" she asks. Spoken like a true wife and mother.

Not necessarily. I have, on occasion, suggested an "arrangement" in which the mother and I would live apart but legally share custody, expenses, etc.

"How's that going?"

So far, I say, no one has taken me up on my offer. And I expect that, the older I get, the less likely it is that someone will.

"Ah." She looks pained for me.

I'm Waiting for the Day

"How come you didn't contact me sooner?"

Too scared. Scared you wouldn't respond. Scared you'd say, No. Scared you'd say, Yes. Scared you would say (as my friend Beth has said), "I acknowledge the special relationship that we had—and I remember you fondly—but I've moved on with my life, and I think it's time that that you do, too."

"So what gave you the courage?"

My father's death. After coping with that, I felt that I could deal with anything. And, of course, there was this book idea that I wanted to talk to you about.

"I almost forgot. What's going on with that? Have you written something? Do you have an agent or a publisher?"

I tell her that I have an agent, but no publisher, and I've already completed a detailed proposal.

"Without an ending?" she asks.

It's all about the journey.

"What if there is no book?"

No book?

"What if it is never published?"

Well then, I say, I will continue to live on in poverty, obscurity, and loneliness until I get the courage to put a bullet through my head.

"I think I preferred the wiseass answer," she says.

U Can't Touch This

We stare at each other for a good, long while. Then, she gestures with her right hand—as if to say, "What are you gonna do?"—and carries off, with the side of her palm, the bowl of her wine glass . . . up and away from the table . . . tumbling over and spilling its contents . . .

Whoa! I jump back out of harm's way. In a splash, the front of her beige blouse is drenched in the house red. Punishment from the gods? A mischievous message from home? Who cares. The tension shatters (especially when the glass lands on the table intact and upright), and we pour laughter.

I offer a napkin—with my hand attached—to her offended bosom. She takes the napkin, and shoos my paw. Then she shakes off the dashing waiter.

"No, thanks, really," she says to his offer of club soda. Briefly daubing some water on the widening stain, she chuckles. "No big deal. Just my favorite blouse."

She remains calm and seated, doesn't get up for at least

another half hour. Right there is another reason I was so fond of her: Swipe, daub, and done . . . and back into the conversational current. If it were me, and my beloved shirt, I'd have been hysterically trying to wrangle the entire wait and bus staff, looking for a dozen rolls of paper towels and an all-night dry cleaner.

Maybe that's another by-product of being a mother: you take accidents and spills in stride.

Shit happens.

God Only Knows (Reprise)

Friday, 10:48 PM–11:28 PM

We share some blueberry pie (no worries about getting that on her blouse) for dessert, and talk for another hour. But, for all intents and purposes, the fat lady has shouted.

We wind down, though, with some heavy stuff.

She tells me about a late-night call from the hospital: Her (then) 16-year-old son had been in an accident. He was unconscious.

"We rushed over in an absolute panic."

I can't imagine what that trip was like.

"When we got there, the doctors told us: 'We don't know if he'll make it through the night.'"

No parent could be equipped to hear those words. What did you do?

"Cried. Prayed. Made all kinds of bargains with God. Found out, maybe, if there's a God or not."

Is there?

"I have to believe He was there that night."

I followed with my own near-death tale: Class-five

whitewater rafting on the notorious Cherry Creek run of the Upper Tuolumne (outside of Yosemite) in California. It was after the breakup with Francine, and I went alone.

Around the trip's midpoint, at a spot named Christmas Hole, our boat got turned and flipped—three of the four paddlers were thrown into the froth. I was sucked into a hydraulic—*the hole*—while the freezing water sucked all the breath out of me. Which was fine, because I couldn't move anyway. The surface was three feet above me, but I was stuck solid in the vise of the vortex.

"What did you do?"

I flailed away for what seemed like hours—it was probably about ten or 12 seconds—and then just stopped. I realized there was nothing more I could do, and that I was probably going to die in this wild, scary place 3,000 miles from home.

Then the river spit me up and out. It wasn't my place or time. Everyone was retrieved safely, and we finished the run without incident or even discussion. Afterward, I called my parents to tell them that I was fine. They, of course, had no reason to assume otherwise. I just wanted to hear the voices of some people who cared if I lived or died.

"That reminds me," she says before hurrying to the ladies' room. "I have to get going," she says. "Bill is gonna kill me."

I'll Be Seeing You

Friday, 11:57 PM

It's nearly midnight, a light rain spitting down, when a cab pulls up for her.

It was great to see you, I say. Let's do it again some time soon.

"Yes," she says. "Let's."

We lean in for a quick hug, her red-blooded chest seeming to slightly recoil from the embrace. We kiss air, which tastes like cool water. I wave as the cab spins off and up the avenue. I walk the next two blocks slowly, but still make it home by 12. I know that's supposed to mean something in fairy tales, but I can't recall what.

8

They Can't Take That Away from Me

The following day, I receive this e-mail message:

From: Sarah F
Sent: Saturday 10:07 AM

```
A casual passerby might have thought it was red
wine, but there was no doubt: blood was
spilled. Wounds were opened or, at the very
least, revealed. In the wake of morning, what
did she feel? Pain. Relief. Exhilaration.
Mostly ambivalence.
Twenty-five years later she was (a lot) older,
somewhat wiser and, hopefully, far more
compassionate. If there is one thing that
motherhood teaches, it is selflessness. But
there she was, listening to a story, partly her
story, partly not. A story in which she was
largely the villain (or at least that's how she
perceived it).
```

Was she still being selfish just by being there?
The things revealed were from the heart, but
perhaps she was lying to herself. She truly
does not know.
She does not remember ever apologizing for the
casualties she caused. Hopefully, it isn't too
late . . . She is truly sorry.
Where her life will lead seems rather certain.
She made choices and lives with them with
little regret. Some may see it as settling;
she does not. Besides, not all soul mates must
be life mates (not necessarily in this life
anyway).
She had two great loves. One she married, one
she did not.
To be continued . . .

If My Friends Could See Me Now

It's a week later. (I think. All of these cuts and time changes are confusing the hell out of me.) In addition to most of the core Boys, our visiting Brit, Martin, makes it in for this Night. They are eager to know how it went . . . and how it is going.

"C'mon," Chung says, "spill your guts."

I spill.

There is not a dry glass in the house.

"Unbelievable." Phil.

"Incredible." Beth.

"Good for you." Andy.

"Brilliant." Martin.

"Schmuck."

What *is* your problem, Gerry?

"I'm not sure what good can come of this. What about her husband?"

He's fine, I say. They'll probably go into counseling.

"And that's it?" Gerry says. "What happens now? You drop into her life, create havoc, and then poof, everything is fine. For you, maybe. Not for her. Certainly not for Bill. "

"Gerry," Phil interrupts. "Why is this thing such a big deal to you? Why do you identify so much with this woman's husband?"

"Gerry?" Phil repeats.

"My dad," Gerry says.

Gerry's father, Emilio, was 85 when he died two years ago; Roz, his mother, at 80, passed away ten months later. Gerry idolized his father and admitted he "never really liked my mother."

We are about to find out why.

Desolation Row

"Twenty-four years ago," Gerry says, "my older sister found a letter in my mother's drawer—I don't know what she was doing snooping around in there—from a man, not my father, writing about some, shall we say, intimate moments. The letter was postmarked from the town where my mother grew up, and the date on it was recent. My sister and I confronted my mother, who calmly informed us, 'Yes, I have been seeing another man, my high school sweetheart, for a number of years. Your father has not been interested in me sexually since you'— meaning me—'were born. This man was widowed young, and he reached out to me soon after his wife passed away. We will never discuss this matter again, and if you say anything to your father, you will both be banished from this home without a penny. And be assured that we *will* leave all of our money to charity when we die.'

"Neither my sister or I ever said a word to my father," Gerry continues. "We had no idea if the story about his sex drive was true—my dad was too honorable a man ever to cheat—but we both agreed that it would be too hurtful for him to know under any circumstances. When my mother died, her estate was worth millions. We ended up donating most of it to charity; it seemed to us too much like blood money. I've always regretted not telling my father, and I will never forgive my mother."

What are the odds that the same scenario would be repeated in the son's life by *his* wife? Fifty-fifty? Sixty-Forty? Considering how much Gerry identified with his father, the poor guy never had a chance.

Andy breaks the long silence. "Sorry, Ger, I didn't know."

"Jeez, that's tough, pal." Chung.

"Unbelievable." Phil.

"Incredible." Beth.

"You guys!" Martin.

> **MARTIN,** 61, 6'; 192 lbs. (13.7 stone); balding, bearded, salt-and-pepper-haired movie producer and financial advisor who lives in his native London with his American wife and young daughter, rarely offers much insight into his interior life, but is by far our most ebullient and appreciative audience member. He will follow a spectacularly personal revelation, funny or sad, with a rich laugh and the hearty encomium, "You guys!" (which really means: "You goofy Yanks!").

"I don't mean to be insensitive," says Robert, "but can we get back to the topic at hand." Looking at me, he asks a typical shrink question: "How do *you* feel after your encounter with Sarah?"

And the Healing Has Begun

- I feel like a much freer man than I was before this whole process began.

- I feel grateful to Sarah for responding so forthrightly and bravely to my questions and comments.

- I feel validated, not only by someone else—but by *the* someone—who confirmed that it happened pretty much as I imagined it did.

- I feel vindicated by sticking to my story, undeterred by external or internal voices.

- I feel stronger (but not harder) for having been broken (but not killed).

- I feel like an explorer who's seen the dual forces of God and Nature, Past and Present, Being and Nothingness, and Love and Solitude converge and collide.

"Whoa, Hemingway," says Beth, using her favorite (if slightly sarcastic) nickname for me. "You might want to tone down that last bit. The critics might not get that you're joking."

I Can Let Go Now

My emotional arc is nearly complete.

- A huge burden has been lifted.
- I am sanguine with my life choices.
- I am a better man for having contacted, seen, and spoken to Sarah.

"Have you shown her any material you've written thus far?" asks Chung.

Yeah, I sent her about 30 pages.

"What did she think?"

Ain't She Sweet

From: Sarah F

Sent: Wednesday 10:47 PM

"A heartwarming journey into the most private recesses of the mind. *The One That Got Away* is honest, poignant and poetic. The imagery is so rich that one feels like a character in the story. Mr. Schreiber wields the keyboard like a scalpel, skillfully exposing the raw nerves in all of us. This young (okay, middle-aged) writer has a bestseller on his hands."

—**Sarah B-F** (I've always wanted to do that hyphenated thing)

"I'd give all my thumbs to see this movie."

—**Ebert**

```
[no reply yet]
```
—Siskel

```
"The passage about cellulite made us weep."
```
—The Editors, AARP Magazine

```
"I suppose now I can't run for public office.
. . . Thanks, Mom."
```
—Barbara F [Sarah's daughter], **Yale Law
School, Class of 2006**

```
"No good can come of this."
```
—Bill F [Sarah's husband]

"Brilliant," says Martin.

"Clever," says Chung, an editor of business books. "But what did she really think?"

From: Sarah F
Sent: Wednesday 2:22 PM

```
So what did I really think of the proposal?
I am incredibly impressed, but not the least
bit surprised. I never doubted your talent,
only the ability to earn a living with it.
I am most amazed by two things: 1. the
musicality (is that a word?) of the language—
the way some sentences soar like symphonies,
while others are lowdown dirty like delta blues
(by the way, I did catch your sly use of song
titles in every heading and subhead); and
2. your memory.
My short-term memory is okay, but my long-term
memory is awful. Therefore, I can't always
```

confirm that your recollections are 100 percent accurate; they seem to be, for the most part.

• I certainly remember the first dance and the invisible cigarette (that was the hook that got me), but I surely don't remember what either of us were wearing.

• I definitely don't remember speaking about my parents that night (the dialogue sounds a little contrived), and I wasn't quite a change-of-life baby . . . simply unplanned.

• I surely remember the two weeks playing house, but I don't remember the naked high-heeled thing;

• And, more recently, I ordered the house Cabernet Sauvignon (I don't like Merlot).

The story is easy to follow, and not just because I know most of it by heart. I am flattered by much, but not all, of what you've written. (I know that Annette Funicello was "the teen goddess" for many of you baby boomer boys, but I much prefer the comparisons to contemporary girls such as Jennifer Connelly and Natalie Portman.)
I particularly like the way you integrate our e-mail conversations, but I do hope that you will use discretion in deleting particularly personal details; I'd hate to have to sue your ass.

```
I eagerly await more material. I'm especially
interested to find out how it ends . . .
```

Words Get in the Way

"She's not a bad writer," says Phil, a literary agent.

Who knew?

"You should give her a chapter to write," says Phil. "It'll offer an opportunity to show the same story from another perspective."

Good idea, I say.

"I hate to burst your bubble, buddy," says Gerry, still hoisting his keenest scabbard. "But I guarantee her tone—and her tune—will change drastically when she realizes how much this could adversely affect her marriage."

Gerry, old pal, I respond, you are probably right.

And that thought, of actually having to cajole and discuss and negotiate—with an agent, a publisher, *and* her—is too exhausting to even contemplate. So I say: I'm beat, Boys. Thanks, as always, for being there. Let's call it a night.

"Just one more thing," says Beth.

What?

"What about *us*? Do you think we could help write a chapter? Maybe a short one?"

How about half of one?

More than Words

It is a while before I have any new "book" material to send Sarah. It takes more time than I'd anticipated to sift through all the rich, teeming, pregnant personal and professional material that results from our re-connection. We make vague plans to have brunch in the near future, but there seem to be a raft of respective issues, dilemmas, and scheduling problems that need to be sorted out before something can be finalized.

After the reunion dinner, we correspond almost daily, ignoring minutiae in a grander attempt to help each other overcome the major impediments that seem to be preventing us, respectively, from enjoying the fullness of our lives.

My missives tend to be shorter and more contained, but quite illuminating regarding the insidious effects of a nostalgia disorder with a predisposition toward obsessive analysis. Sarah's less-calculated, lengthier monologues provide (at least) a chapter's worth of material detailing the escalating confusion, faltering resolution and equivocating certitude of a middle-aged woman who's been involuntarily forced to reevaluate the major choices she's made in her adult life. (Below are the significant e-mails, beginning with our immediate back-and-forth discourse; then focusing mainly on her changing, shifting points of view (edited, of course, with discretion.)

Say You, Say Me

From: Lee S
Sent: Saturday 4:03 PM

```
i had little clue that we had been talking for
5-1/2 hours until you said you had to go. i'm
still processing the entire evening, so i'm not
sure yet if i've entered some brave new
territory or just traveled a long distance to
```

return to the same place. metaphors aside, did
you get home okay?

From: Sarah F
Sent: Saturday 5:08 PM

I got home fine last night (morning). Bill was
waiting up, and we had a brief chat.
He was none too thrilled about my getting home
after 1 AM. Nor was he too keen on us having
future "private" meetings without him. He said:
"Nothing good will come of it." I tried to
explain why this was different than the time he
contacted his first love, Roberta (and didn't
tell me until months later), but he just
doesn't get it. He did say, however, that he'd
be willing to be interviewed about his "Ones."

From: Lee S
Sent: Sunday 10:35 AM

in fairness to your husband, no one "gets"
anyone else completely; that's why we have
friends, acquaintances, radio call-in hosts,
certified shrinks and (certifiable) ex-
boyfriends.

From: Sarah F
Sent: Tuesday 7:08 PM

I picked up my blouse from the cleaners today,
and most of the blood, I mean wine, came out
. . . Is that some sort of a sign? And, if so,
what does it mean?

From: Lee S
Sent: Friday 5:57 PM

just think: a week ago today we met for the
first time in god-knows-how-many years.
thanks again. i really appreciate your gameness
... that you were so open and honest from the
start, and had no objection to opening your
life to possible (pseudonymous) scrutiny.
it feels as if our reunion did take a great
weight off of me ... and, as a result, i'm
obsessing less about things in which i have
little or no control. what about you?

The Weight

From: Sarah F
Sent: Friday 10:01 PM

I'm glad that you seem to have gotten some
closure. I have always been a proponent of
weight loss (and have spent most of my life in
service of that goal). However, since last

week, I've definitely gotten *heavier* (more in mind, thankfully, than body). Our meeting has forced me to take a look at things I've been avoiding for a long, long time. The more questions I ask, the more weight I seem to acquire.

I really enjoyed being able to converse so freely with you on Friday night. I was surprised how much there was to discuss and, especially, how much I had to say. A while ago I guess I gave up trying to make Bill understand me (and I imagine he's done the same).

I don't know why I have such trouble accepting the people I love for being who they are, and not someone I want them to be. I didn't accept you. I didn't accept Bill. And there have been times when I didn't accept my own children. It's not one of my finer qualities.

From: Sarah F
Sent: Wednesday 10:29 AM

I just wanted you to know that I've read and re-read the passages you sent . . . I think they're really good (but I may be biased). What about finding a publisher?

From: Lee S
Sent: Thursday 9:16 PM

funny you should ask. my agent just called. he
said we have a meeting next tuesday at a major
house (corporate publishing, inc.). the publisher,
some executives and editors want to make sure i
can look and speak good enough for *oprah*.

From: Sarah F
Sent: Monday 3:29 PM

Good luck tomorrow at your meeting. We can deal
with my second thoughts another time.

From: Lee S
Sent: Monday 4:16 PM

what second thoughts?

From: Sarah F
Sent: Monday 5:14 PM

I was just kidding. Knock 'em dead.

From: Lee S
Sent: Tuesday 2:16 PM

the meeting at corporate publishing was
extraordinary.
according to my agent, "it went as well as we

could have possibly hoped." it sure as hell was
gratifying for me . . . to be in a roomful of
14 smart, savvy and attractive publishing
people (10 of whom were women) who only wanted
to talk about me and my work. they all seemed
to have read the material, really *got* it, and
were eager to ask questions . . . about you,
me, the boys . . .
what could be better?
afterward, the acquiring editor came up to me
and said, "it's not a question of 'if'
[there'll be an offer], only 'how much.' "
there was one interesting twist: all along, we
were assuming that this was a "guy" story. but
the women's enthusiastic reaction made us
rethink that strategy. and, as you know, women
make up the bulk of book buyers.
the entire discussion was heartening (not least
of which was the money—at least six figures,
they intimated).
sorry to monopolize the discussion, but i
haven't been this excited over a meeting since
. . . well, never.
how're you doing? no need for those second
thoughts. i promised you that no material would
be printed if you strongly object to it . . .
and (as long as you don't unreasonably withhold
approval) my word is good.

From: Sarah F
Sent: Tuesday 5:27 PM

I guess I'm just going to have to sue your ass.
No, seriously, I'm very happy for you. You've

worked long and hard. You deserve some fame and
fortune. And, just think, if things keep
deteriorating in my home, you could get a real
blockbuster ending.
My life is pretty much an open book to you,
and I don't much care what others think of my
role in this drama (not that I'm anxious to be
portrayed as a heartless, manipulative bitch).
But I still reserve the right to protect the
innocent (like my family, who did not agree to
be a part of this endeavor).

From: Lee S
Sent: Tuesday 10:48 PM

you know that i would never do anything to hurt
you or your family, and my intention has never
been to break up your marriage. honest.
what do you mean about things "deteriorating in
my home"? what's going on?

She Said, She Said

From: Sarah F
Sent: Wednesday 7:58 AM

I don't believe it was/is your intent to break
up my marriage, and I didn't weather 20-plus
years of wedded bliss to walk away from it in
confusion. On the other hand, after all this
time, my husband and I still have a great deal

of difficulty accepting one another. I am a
rather stubborn woman. I am not, nor have I
ever been, the dutiful, supportive wife that he
would have liked.
Sometimes we feel that we've tortured each
other enough. Mostly we don't think about it
(that's why we're still married).

From: Sarah F
Sent: Thursday 3:19 PM

Seeing you has brought up lots of unresolved
feelings at a time when I'm not too secure
about very much in my life. As the days have
gone by since our meeting, I find myself
checking my e-mail several times a day with a
schoolgirl's nervousness. I told you that I've
never been unfaithful in my marriage, but these
feelings have made me feel guilty… like I've
been sneaking around. (We both know that part
of being a grown-up is not necessarily acting
on every feeling you have.)
My guilt has made me somewhat of a bitch at
home.

From: Sarah F
Sent: Monday 9:43 AM

I'm really not sure exactly what it is we (you
and I) are doing. I would like to believe that
we are "old" (well not that old) friends

catching up on years gone by ... But I don't think it's as simple as that (speaking only for myself of course), and that uncertainty has colored most of the past two and a half weeks. I have been alternately relentless and bitchy (not my best qualities), and I'm not sure to what end.

From: Sarah F
Sent: Tuesday 11:31 AM

I wonder if I am subconsciously (or not so subconsciously) preventing things between Bill and me from getting better.
I am still trying to determine what role you play, if any, in my current situation at home. Whatever else there is between us, you represent the other side of the choices I've made.
When we were together in our youth, part of me wanted to be with you as a "writer" (being different, non-materialistic, etc.), but a bigger part of me wanted a doctor or lawyer [a wish shared by my mother and father as well—*lrs*] with the house in the suburbs, 2 kids and a dog. Well, the house is a noose around my neck, the kids are grown, and the dog pisses/shits on everything.
I've clearly got to get a better handle on this confusion, and a better grip on myself.

From: Sarah F
Sent: Thursday 5:36 PM

I finally made an appointment with a shrink; I'm
seeing her tonight. Whatever confusion, conflict
or problems I'm having at home, in my marriage
and my head . . . I need someone who's
qualified to help resolve them.

From: Sarah F
Sent: Friday 6:58 PM

I liked the shrink very much. She's a little
new-agey, but she seems to listen and talk (I
didn't want a therapist who constantly meets
your question with a question; I prefer someone
who is more proactive.)
My issues were present long before you
reappeared. But I won't be naïve enough to
think that your presence has not put them in a
new perspective.
I guess we (you and I) kept coming back to
each other because something was lost without
the other . . . that we were not complete. I
suppose that's why I feel you are my soul mate.
Something is always missing without you.
The question now is: Can we maintain a platonic
friendship with this knowledge? Or is Bill
right when he says, "Nothing good will come of
it." I've never been much of a gambler, but I'm
willing to stay in the game . . . as long as
the stakes don't get too high.

From: Sarah F
Sent: Monday 10:58 AM

Things blew up this weekend on my home front.
Not the first time, probably not the last . . .
and nothing was resolved. We've replayed this
scenario many times in 25 years . . . lots of
hurt feelings and anger expressed. Maybe that's
what they mean by "till death do us part."

From: Sarah F
Sent: Thursday 3:19 PM

For the past month, it seems as if I've been
pushing Bill to take some action so I don't
have to make some hard decisions. As you know,
I've always been a bit of a coward.
I'll openly admit, if Bill and I had not been
together, I probably would have contacted you
at some point . . . I would have wanted to
connect and yes, maybe live together
(figuratively speaking), though I'm pretty sure
I'd never want to get married again.
Would we last? I have no idea, though I'm damn
sure if it ended, it would not be for the same
reasons as before.

From: Sarah F
Sent: Monday 9:04 AM

Another tumultuous weekend . . . beginning with
a huge fight on Friday night. I won't bore you

with all of the details. But we didn't speak
for the next 24 hours . . . until Bill sat me
down and asked, "How would you feel if I left?"
This led to a four-hour discussion rehashing
our many problems.
Sunday morning, Bill acted as though nothing
had happened (I don't forget so quickly). Later
on, he brought home a new Taylor guitar (a
beauty, something I've always wanted) for me,
and told me that he still loved me. I really
do love Bill in many ways; he is a good human
being, father and husband ... but I don't know
if I'm prepared to go on with business as usual.
Maybe I'm not ever going to be fully satisfied
with anyone . . . or maybe I'm too stubborn
and selfish to make anyone else truly happy.
(You remember these self-pitying jags of mine?)
What a catch!

From: Sarah F
Sent: Wednesday 5:36 PM

Bill and I begin our first couples' counseling
session tonight. (If you're keeping score at
home, that's Couples therapy on Wednesday and
Individual on Thursday).
I'm not sure when I'll be free to get together
with you again. I might have one, possibly two,
available Sundays over the next several months.
Last night in counseling (I like this shrink,
too) Bill expressed increasingly annoyance at
our (yours and my) daily correspondence . . .
and my preoccupation with it/you. He would like

the *three* of us to get together and "be friends."

So Complicated

Whew. My brain is spinning with the impact of her yo-yoing thoughts, feelings, and moods. While trying to stay level and calm (and encouraging her to do the same), I don't feel that I'm qualified to offer specific advice. Besides, how can I truly be objective?

She is obviously in some pain, and I feel badly. Even if I did not create the whole bloody mess, I certainly added more than a grain of salt.

I tell her, I am not yet up for a "threesome" with Bill; I am not sure what point—or whose benefit—that would serve. But I'm glad she took my advice to get some professional counseling.

There's not much more I can do. So I suggest that we take a few days off—from each other. I use the time to get involved in some *other* folks' lives.

To: Andy, Beth, Chung . . .
Sent: Sunday 9:01 AM

how're you doing? what's going on in your life?

(FYI: I do not send out a group mailing; I individualize each missive. I'm a much better friend than that.)

Beth, bless her heart, puts aside her own issues to compose a penetrating, perceptive, perspicacious, and perspective-placing analysis of recent events.

From: Beth B
Sent: Tuesday 8:36 AM

Hemingway,
No need to beat up on yourself or feel guilty
about Sarah's home strife. She was already at a
point in her life where she was questioning her
life choices. Your reappearance only
accelerated the process.
You could not have known how your presence
would affect her or her marriage. I certainly
did not expect it. No one did. She believes you
emerged at this time because of fate. You're
not responsible for fate.
You were each other's first great loves, and
maybe soul mates, but at 23 she painlessly
moved on because she was pragmatic and saw the
life she wanted . . . a traditional marriage,
with kids, and a house in the suburbs ... all
the things that women are conditioned to want.
She may have saved your letters and thought
about you from time to time, but she was too
busy dealing with her day-to-day life to do
more than that.
More recently, with her kids out of the house,
she's had more time to question her choices.
She's had more time to think about what's
missing, and what she's missed by choosing the
life she did.
How could you have known that at the same time

you were doing your detective work she was embarking on a quest of her own? She was trying to track down the moment that her life got lost, and if (and how) she could get it back on course.

Now, she is faced with another life . . . yours . . . which she seems to have idealized. (If she only knew.) Of course, in any comparison, her good old reliable husband doesn't have a fair shot. You've got a double-sided edge . . . her fond memory of a moody, idealistic young man; and the romanticized perception of a middle-aged, still-struggling-but-never-say-die writer.

No matter what we (men and women) say, we all want, at least a little bit, what we don't have.

In the end, I'm betting she will probably find her way back home . . . and you will have found the answers that will enable you to move on. And, if you're both smart, you'll be thankful for the choices you've made and find satisfaction in them.

Life ain't perfect. You're certainly not. So start there, accepting yourself for who you are (and who you're not) . . . and remain vulnerable to all of life's possibilities.

Love,

Beth

Beth's input, which is sound, valid, and greatly appreciated, pushes my own taxed, fragilely teetering brain into synapse overload. Sleep deprivation fries the remaining terminals clear through.

As a result, my exhaustion begets extreme . . . um . . . confusion. I am... uh . . . not . . . processing information . . . as quick . . . ah . . . ly as usual. My thinking . . . becomes . . . is . . . uh . . . What am I thinking? Not clearly . . . The thought (is that how to spell *thought*? Not *thaught*?) processesesees are . . . very foggy . . . and distorted . . . and, as a result . . . I may have said . . . and done . . . some . . . um . . . foolish things . . .

9

Days Like This

Another One Bites the Dust

From: John Smith [my literary agent]
To: Lee S
Sent: Monday 2:42 PM

I have been waiting for my anger to subside before writing you. As I believe you now realize, your e-mail to Joe Jones, president of Corporate Publishing, Inc. was a very serious breach of etiquette. Your persistence in pushing forward in such a hell-bent manner without consulting me is hurtful to our agency's best representation of your work, and hurtful to my reputation.

I respect you as a writer, and I respect the book that we have set out to work on together, but I spent a restless night deciding that I think you would be best served by finding other representation. I will willingly furnish you with a list of other editors who will likely be very interested in the new proposal, but I

suggest that you find new representation before
approaching them.
I'm sorry that it came to this, but life is
too short to mince feelings or words. I think
that moving on is in both our interests.
Best,
John Smith [my former agent]

Ah, yes, it is all coming back to me.

I'm sure that I am not the first temporarily (or even permanently) addled writer ever to directly contact the head of a
publishing house in the wake of a stunning rejection. And
John S., a decent fellow, is just doing his job. Business is business, and I understand that he'll do a lot more business with
the company in question than he could possibly hope to do by
representing me.

What was I thinking when I began drafting the above-men-
tioned (see below) letter to the president? Well, as I mentioned
last chapter, I wasn't thinking all that clearly. At the dawn after
a sleepless night, I was convinced that if I did nothing, I had
zero chance to alter fate; whereas, if I took a 100,000-to-1 shot,
then at least I'd have that one slim possibility. (Yes, I actually
thought that it was *possible* I could change this executive's
mind.)

At 5 AM, my mind seemed so lucid and energized with a
proactive attitude to address and redress what was obviously a
churlish and capricious decision. Instead of absorbing and in-
ternalizing the rejection, I was accepting responsibility for it.
And by doing *something* to reverse it, I was refusing to feel vic-
timized by circumstances out of my control.

You play the cards you're dealt, right?

No question, I may have been handed pure *dreck*, but if I

acted decisively and quickly, I could (*just maybe, dammit!*) re-think and redirect that decision.

It seemed like such a good idea at the time.

To: Joe Jones
From: Lee S
Sent: Friday 5:53 AM

Dear Mr. Jones:
You just passed on my non-fiction book proposal,
THE ONE THAT GOT AWAY. In what I'm guessing is
not an unprecedented request from a would-be
author, I'm going to make a brief case on why
you should reconsider.
My understanding is that you did not get it
("it" being the idea, the presentation and/or
the commercial viability of the project). I
have no argument there. You're entitled to your
opinion. But it is, I respectfully contend, at
odds with most of the editors working under
your company's banner.
A few weeks ago, I met with more than a dozen
Corporate Publishing staffers, representing all
ages, genders, levels of experience and
influence. It was an extraordinary meeting, a
writer's wet dream, packed with mostly
passionate, smart women who all seemed to have
thoroughly read and responded to the proposal.
They all knew someone, or something, that had
gotten away.
Unanimity was reached at the end of the
meeting: If I could address, and revise, a few
sticking points—among others, to craft a more

female-friendly protagonist and a boffo ending
(acknowledging that non-fiction did have its
realistic constraints)—we would likely have a
deal.

More serendipity: a front-page article in the
Boston Globe on the same subject (boomers
seeking, finding and, in many instances,
rekindling old, true loves) was printed *on the
very day* that your editorial board was
convening to evaluate my revised proposal. A
deal, I was again told, was imminent. But,
apparently, your house had another floor—with
another smaller (acquisitions) board—that
needed to sign off on all recommendations. From
what sources have leaked, yours was the lone
"nay" vote: You just didn't get it.

Again, Mr. Jones, I can't persuade you to like
or even understand this proposal. But I'm sure
that hasn't stopped you from buying a book
before . . . certainly if: 1) your people are
enthusiastically behind it; and 2) it makes
practical, fiscal sense. The *Globe* article
reported that perhaps ten million people over
the age of 35 have contacted their past
girlfriends/boyfriends. Desires are being
fulfilled. Marriages are being tested. A trend
is being uncovered. And whatever you may think
of my manuscript, it can quickly can tap into,
and advance the coverage of, this trend.

It's unseemly to beg for a dime—or, in this
case, $100,000—a pittance by corporate (and
Corporate's) standards. I suspect that your
board spends twice as much on its annual coffee
budget.

You wonder: If I'm such a hot property with no shortage of suitors, why would I even continue to pursue such an uninterested object of desire?
Because I think [Corporate Publishing, Inc.] is the right home for this book. [Jim Jackson] is the right editor. [Bea Faber] is the right publisher. And, if you're as savvy and tough a president as I've heard, and brave enough to rectify a mistake, you're the right executive.
Thank you for your time.
Sincerely,

Start All over Again

Schmuck.

Only a schmuck could entertain the notion (at the crack of dawn no less) that he could craft a letter so persuasive that it would convince a savvy, tough publishing executive to reopen and redress a dead issue that was already buried and forgotten.

Only a schmuck would allow the frustrations built up over 20 years—and more than 365 days working on this particular project—to obscure the self-destructive aspect of such a quixotic correspondence.

Only a schmuck would allow his own distress to delay the on-going correspondence to one who has been so steadfast and supportive during much of this process.

Only a schmuck's sulking would prompt the following message.

From: Sarah F
To: Lee S
Sent: Thursday 9:19 AM
Subject: The What's-Up Questionnaire

Please answer all questions completely and honestly. Check either Yes or No and respond with a comment wherever you see fit. If you prefer not to answer or the question is not applicable simply write "not applicable" or "prefer not to answer" in the comments section. All information provided is strictly confidential.

1. Are you okay? Yes_____ No_____
Comment_____

2. Are you suffering from writer's block?
Yes_____ No_____
Comment_____

3. Are you bored? Yes_____ No_____
Comment_____

4. Are you disinterested (I guess the correct term is "uninterested")?
Yes_____ No_____
Comment_____

5. Suffering from amnesia? Yes_____ No_____
Comment_____
Suffering from denial? Yes_____ No_____
Comment_____
Additional Comments_____

Thank you for participating in this survey.

All Things Must Pass (Reprise)

I completed the survey and added these additional comments:

From: Lee S
Sent: Thursday 2:42 PM

my silence these past few days has nothing to
do with any boredom, denial or lack of interest
on my part. you've been nothing but candid and
open, and i don't want to discourage that level
of communication.
the reason i haven't responded is a
preoccupation with my own travails. it seems
your life may not be an open book, after all.
even though the editorial board of corporate
publishing, inc. recommended making an offer
for the book, the acquisitions board "passed"
(that's publishing-speak for: "don't bother us
with your esoteric little story unless you can
guarantee a spot on *oprah*). no reason was
given, though it seems that the company
president, joe jones, just "didn't get it."
okay, it happens. what apparently does not
happen is the spurned author contacting the
president directly, asking him to reconsider.
long story short: i never heard from joe jones,
but john smith, my agent, fired me, for behaving
in a "hell-bent manner." he actually was very
nice about it, and even recommended me to
another agent, who agreed to represent me. the
new agent, however, warned of the potentiality
that "the book won't be published at all."

From: Sarah F
Sent: Thursday 9:26 PM

Okay, admittedly this is not good news ... I
was certain you would give me a share of the
royalties . . . and people that slighted me in
the past would have newfound respect for me
. . . and I would be immortalized . . . and oh
I forgot this isn't all about me!
For a guy who has never been one to give all
that much weight to the opinions of others,
your life certainly depends a great deal on the
opinions of others ... Quel irony, huh?
No really, that's gotta suck. I'm sorry.

From: Lee S
Sent: Friday 11:33 PM

thanks for the peppy pep talk. and, again,
apologies for my erratic responses.
sometimes, it's too exhausting to explain
myself, to try and come up with new and
interesting ways to say i'm disappointed,
depressed, whatever . . . without coming across
as a self-absorbent, self-abhorrent whiner.

From: Sarah F
Sent: Saturday 5:55 PM

I'm still having some trouble understanding how
someone I view as such a private person would
be willing to put so much of himself out there

for everyone to see and judge. Why do that, especially if it's not likely to bring you critical or financial rewards?

I consider myself fairly open and honest, mainly because I know that most people aren't paying attention. They're too consumed with their own problems. And the few that are listening? Well, they're probably not taking the time to "get" what I'm trying to say. But your goal is to be understood. You're constantly asking people to judge your words and thoughts.

As I've said before, it seems brave, but very crazy.

Underlying Depression (Melancholia)

From: Sarah F
Sent: Monday 9:48 AM

I hope you will forgive my unsolicited "advice," but as a friend, soul mate, soul sibling or whatever, I can't sit by silently while you are clearly in pain. We're all entitled to our woe is me time (I am the queen of self pity, so I should know). But all good things must come to an end.

What are you doing to get yourself out of this rut? You helped convince me to get "help," so I assume you realize that right now you could use a little help yourself. Are you talking to anyone? How are you filling your days?

This is a time when someone (like Cher in

Moonstruck) has to slap you across the face and shout, "Snap out of it!" . . .
Consider yourself slapped!

From: Sarah F
Sent: Monday 3:28 PM

Come on, cheer up!

From: Lee S
Sent: Tuesday 1:11 AM

ah, yes: the snap-out-of-it, cheer-up approach to depression. works every time.
apparently I'll forgive you anything, even unsolicited advice. and while i do appreciate the thought (and 1 or 2 of your other suggestions), the last thing a person like me wants to hear is some version of: "snap out of it."
depression may be triggered by outside events, but its cognitive core is mysteriously calibrated by several key chemicals—some of which are missing, some of which are rife but out of balance . . . it takes years of mostly trial and error to find the right mix of drugs and talk therapy (and then, almost overnight, these measures can prove ineffectual). for those individuals suffering from severe

depression (which, thankfully, is not my
problem), the proper balance may never be
found.

i don't mind you slapping me around or telling
me to snap out of it. i would do the same if i
saw someone in my condition. but let me share a
little-known secret: that response *never* works.
more often, it has the opposite effect, leaving
the slapee feeling even more alone and
despairing. he knows he's stuck. he doesn't
need to be snapped or slapped as a reminder.

From: Sarah F
Sent: Tuesday 9:59 AM

Okay, so maybe "snap out of it" wasn't exactly
the most nurturing advice, but it seems to have
worked . . . a little. At least you're showing
a little fight.

I know it must be difficult for you. But I
really believe you'll find someone in publishing
who understands the universality of this
subject and believes in your unique approach to
it.

Though it might not be the greatest thing for
my life, I do want it to happen for your sake…
and, of course, for the reading public.

If you ever need me, I will try to be there
for you.

From: Lee S
Sent: Wednesday 1:06 AM

thanks for your thoughtful message. it didn't
make me feel much better, but it didn't make me
feel any worse.
my wallow must be nearing its end. i have taken
a few steps (i made a phone call) to get some
work, and i am sufficiently out of myself to
genuinely be concerned about others.
how are *you* doing?

The Circle Game

From: Sarah F
Sent: Wednesday 9:16 AM

Okay, good. We can now return to the
rollercoaster/soap opera that is my life.
The storm clouds at home are building again. A
lot of issues are coming up in *both* therapy
sessions. I wonder if Bill and I can ever get
past our anger.
Control is another big issue. It's so pervasive
in our marriage. Every time we eat out, Bill
asks me where I want to go. And after I
answer, he then counters with, "Well, what
about . . . ?"
Am I being unreasonable, or should he know me
better by now?

The One That Got Away

From: Sarah F
Sent: Wednesday 4:41 PM

You busy working . . . or moping? (I know you
hate these questions, but I just want to make
sure you don't regress back into your shell.)
I wanted to clarify a few more thoughts about
love and marriage.

Bill and I probably have different definitions
for the word "love" (as it pertains to
marriage). I believe he has more of a pragmatic
attitude. I do not. I wanted us to be
everything to one another. Right from the
start, he wanted something else . . . He wanted
a lot of time with the guys: Friday nights
drinking; Sundays playing softball; etc. While
we were dating I didn't make a big deal about
it, though I did express my displeasure with
the Friday night thing. I suppose I thought it
would change after we were married.

It never did, and my resentment only built up
over the years. And, of course, the more my
disappointment showed, the more angry he
became. He, too, feels that he was sold a bill
of goods (so to speak) . . . that I acted one
way when we were dating, and then began acting
differently when we got married.

At least Bill never represented anything other
than what he was . . .

From: Lee S
Sent: Thursday 11:15 AM

for what it's worth, at no extra cost to you
or your family (not yet, anyway), i'm going to
give you the benefit of my insights, especially
as it relates to a subject about which i know
nothing: marriage.

in my opinion, you've mischaracterized your
nature: i believe you are the pragmatic one. it
seems to me that you went into your marriage
knowing all along that you weren't going to
receive everything you wanted. as you
indicated, bill never changed his behavior; it
was, instead, your own expectations that became
increasingly unrealistic… and caused you to
become increasingly resentful. why resent
someone who's being true to himself?

do you think it would've been any different
with me? i would've wanted to maintain my
monday night basketball, and my wednesday night
poker, and my sunday softball . . . and i
would have been a very unhappy camper if you
forced me to give them up.

my opinion is: friday night with the boys and
sunday softball games are irrelevant. what is
much more pertinent, and pressing, should be
the communication and understanding you both
seem to lack on the other days and nights of
your lives.

i speak from experience here: bill is not the
cause of your pain; he's just the reminder of
life's disappointments. you've encouraged me to
assume more responsibility for my behavior, and

not take out my resentment on someone else
because i'm depressed or dissatisfied.
it's not bill's fault that he's not who you
want him to be. and if you could stop acting
out, you'd feel a lot better about yourself
(cause you intuitively know that it's unfair
and cowardly). believe me, i do know. i've been
acting out in this way with most of my ex-
girlfriends since . . . well, since you.

From: Sarah F
Sent: Thursday 2:02 PM

I beg to differ with your esteemed opinion
based on your many years of *successful*
relationships. I disagree with your supposition
that Bill and I have a lack of communication. I
think we communicate a lot better than most
couples. We often talk to each other. Where we
may have some difficulty is in understanding,
and perhaps accepting, each other.

From: Lee S
Sent: Thursday 2:38 PM

unless i'm being overly sensitive/defensive,
let me respond with the first thought that comes
to mind: fuck you. it seems to me that you
were somewhat defensive (and nasty) with your
gratuitous shot.
to me, communication is defined by a high level
of understanding and acceptance between
individuals; the fact that people take the time

to talk and/or share their thoughts and feelings is not a barometer of how well they communicate.

From: Sarah F
Sent: Thursday 6:06 PM

Sorry. I apologize for being both defensive and nasty. And you're probably right about the definition of communication. Also, I did go into my marriage knowing that he was not giving me everything I required emotionally. I thought it would change (and yes, I am guilty of that foolish/common belief that you can change people after you marry them).
This was a particularly bad week. I don't know whether my hormones were out of whack or not, but I found myself atypically depressed and withdrawn. I ended up backing Bill into a corner. I can't quite understand this destructive dance we do, but I am beginning to think that most of the problems in our relationship are my doing. I just wish I could figure out why I continue to act out, knowing that nothing positive is ever going to come out of it.
Well, so much for growth and self-awareness.

It's All Too Much

From: Lee S
Sent: Friday 10:40 AM

now that the black dog (as winston churchill
called depression) is limping off in search of
a new master, i've been thinking about your
unsettled situation at home . . . and my part
in it. i believe that my presence has definitely
compounded many of your problems. it's human
nature to question the choices we make,
especially ones made a long, long time ago. but
it's like our roles have reversed, and you're
now idealizing me and what might have been.
when you share intimate details about your
marriage, it does occasionally feel as if we
are having an "emotional" affair . . . and the
more understanding and accepting i am, the less
likely you'll make the effort with bill. so,
even though we've been open, chaste and above
board in our renewed relationship, i think we
should take all the "what-if"s off the table.
it's not fair to you or bill. no 24-7 life can
compete with an exotic vacation fantasy. and,
while *this* vacation might not be any picnic,
it's still exotic.
you've said it yourself: i represent the other
side of the life you've made. and, just like
the trauma of my dad's death initiated my
latest round of soul searching, i believe the
trauma of your marital troubles—and my
opportune reemergence—have made you rethink
your choices.

we're both lousy landscapers. the grass is
always greener . . .
i propose that we officially and definitively
eliminate any possible romantic equation
between us and offer the lamest, but truest,
excuse known to man (and woman): let's remain
friends.
yep, i know, you're thinking: i drop into your
life unbidden, create a world of chaos . . .
and then disappear, via email, no less.
but i'm certainly not disappearing. if
anything, i'm making my presence even more
palpable: i'm here whenever you need me, or
not. nothing changes with our fundamental
friendship. if anything, i'm even more confident
(and content) in the fact that we will always
be there for each other. we have become—again
or, more likely, for the first time—best
friends.

"Jeez ," some of you might be saying, "where did *that* decision come from? It seems awfully presumptuous and precipitous."

Not really. It's been a long time coming.

A good poker player is constantly making split-second determinations that seemingly come from nowhere ("on the one hand . . . and yet, on the other hand . . ."). But, in actuality, the thought process is completed after all factors—empirical (past), situational (present), and instinctual (gut)—have been dutifully and indubitably considered.

So, what *am* I thinking?

King of Wishful Thinking

I am thinking of little else. I am thinking about the last 25 years. And I am thinking, I believe, clearly.

Ever since Sarah and I re-met, my soul has been at war. Or my *souls*. Good/kind/altrustic soul battling vs. Evil/opportunistic/narcissistic soul. Like most homo sapiens, I have a heterogeneous nature that is often in conflict. I see all—or neither—sides of an issue. I want my cake, and I want icing, writing, and candles on it, and I want to pay a fair price for it, and I want to eat it, and I want few caloric consequences.

At the same time, I feel for the cake. I empathize with its place in the food chain, and its desire for a more prominent place at the table.

But I digress.

I think I still love Sarah, whatever that means (though I don't know if I am *in love* with her, whatever that means). I wish her well, and I don't want any hurt or harm to come to her or her family. And I think that I might be contributing to that end, or could possibly end up doing just that while I leer, or even just lurk, around. (I also empathize with Bill, having often found myself on the short end of Sarah's affections.)

I think I still *want* Sarah, but not with the same burning desire as I once did. Call it aging, maturation, or just the scourge of a diminishing libido. When I look at her, I don't get the same gut-flopping, stomach-churning, johnson-hardening sensation of my youth. I see her, and I see me, for who we are: two (too) moody, critical, cracked, sentimental, soulful (in the conflicting-nature sense), imperfect, battle-and-gravity-scarred warriors who will likely never find a separate peace in this world.

On the other hand, reward doesn't come without risk. And this could be the last, best chance to alter the course of human existence (at least, mine). Can I afford to let it to pass with nary a whimper (much less a bang)? Besides, Sarah has matured (in a good way). She's much more responsible and mindful of consequences. She's certainly learned, as a mother, to think first of others. And, after all, hasn't she been faithful for these years?

And yet . . .

A wise woman once said to me, "Not all soul mates must be life mates, not in this life anyway."

In a perfect world, I might be able to escape free and clear—without responsibilities or repercussions. But we don't live there. Here, instead, I've brought considerable turmoil to an entire family that had been minding its own business until I made them part of mine.

It was much simpler when it was just my story. I could manipulate all the characters, and even the conclusion. But when Sarah and her family came aboard, complications multiplied exponentially. Too many personalities—dead and alive—have bustled into our quiet little reunion nook.

We have no choice: We can, and will, always remain true friends and soul mates, but our lives will not otherwise change. She loves her husband and her family too much, while I am still probably married to a bittersweet (albeit happy) ending.

Are my motives pure? Or do I just want what I can't have (and don't want what I can have)? (A clarification: Even though there has never been any serious talk about it, with absolutely no physical contact more than a pecked cheek, I sometimes have the feeling that if I push, scheme, or manipulate during her most vulnerable moments, I might be able to separate Sarah from her bespoke life.)

And if I succeed, then what? Am I prepared to commit myself totally to a married woman? Am I ready and equipped to cope with someone who might, in her next crisis of confidence, return home? Do I want that responsibility? That pressure?

No.

But: We are not dead yet. Older and jowlier, surely, but breathing just the same, thank you.

From: Sarah F
Sent: Friday 6:36 PM

You're breaking up with me? I'm sure my husband
will be happy to hear it (I'm just not sure
if, or when, I'm going to tell him).

10

Taking Care of Business

At the close of the calendar year, Sarah and I take a little break from each other. She goes to San Francisco on business and I remain home to address the vicissitudes of a freelance life:

- Professional Disappointment (still no book deal).
- Personal Dislocation (still no romantic love, or sex).

And then, almost overnight:

- Professional Renaissance (connecting with an "interested" publisher).
- Personal Renewal (bonding with family, friends . . . and at least one unmarried ex).

Workin' for the Man

I won't belabor too many inside-publishing details, only those that are germane to the story: how dismissals and denials can be so injudiciously and off-handedly foisted upon creative, hard-working people; how tastes are subjective; how often we (me and my creative, hard-working friends) have come oh-so-close to a payday-payoff that would have eased the day-to-day struggles; and how little thought and consideration, in the end, is given to *you* the reader (especially to an unconventional reader with catholic tastes and a Yiddish-kiddingish sensibility).

You Can't Always Get What You Want

The preceding paragraph illustrates how easy it is to fall into a miasma of self-pity and self-non-fulfilling prophesy when one spends so much time alone, insulated from human counsel and contact. Though I take full responsibility for my life and my actions, who can doubt that a tendency to say the wrong things to the right people has been additionally amplified by listening solely to the unblocked, uncushioned rattling of one's own thoughts?

And in case any of you sensitive-artiste types have ever pondered: Poverty, seclusion, and dysthymia, individually or collectively, is/are *not* catnip to the ladies.

Out of the Blue

Then again, being unencumbered by salary or spouse can sometimes effect exquisite sensations of *surprise.*

One thing leads to another:

A friend of a friend leads to a meeting with an old acquaintance (now an independent book publisher). "Sure, I'll take a look at your proposal" from the publisher leads to an offer. And my eager confidence/desperation leads me to accept a virtually-no-money-up-front deal with back-end incentives. Which leads to the book in your hands.

A more genial outlook regarding (my) life leads me to contact Connie, a former girlfriend whom I haven't seen or spoken to in a while, but who remains a(n increasingly) fond memory.

> **CONNIE**, 5′3″, 118 lbs.; reddish-brown hair; green eyes; lawyer-turned-makeup person; 14 years my junior; an attractive, smart, funny, sunny, girlish and non-introspective woman when we met (13 months after the death of her father, age 60). However: Instead of merely encouraging her to explore a more examined life, I allowed my own gremlins to channel gratuitously critical comments. As a result, she lost some of her sunniness and girlishness, and I lost track of what attracted her to me in the first place. Still and all, we lasted for three years until finally, out of compassion and self-loathing, I pulled the plug. Soon thereafter, she changed careers, went into group therapy and, typically, became more attractive to me again. Connie, of course, wanted nothing more to do with me. (If she ever thought of me as one that got away, she was soon disabused of that impression.)

I want to believe that enough time has elapsed for her to entertain bygones. And, after all, haven't I become a much kinder, gentler, and more roundly compassionate fellow?

I call on her birthday to wish her well. We have dinner.

She looks great, and sounds just like the sort of smart, funny, sunny, self-aware, and forgiving woman I now covet. But? She is seeing someone. And? She hasn't entirely forgiven me. And? Probably never will.

You Don't Miss Your Water (Till Your Well Runs Dry)

Notice a pattern here? I seem to have sabotaged nearly every significant relationship with overly critical, under-affectionate behavior, likely stemming from the mega-idealization of Sarah, perfect-love incarnate, to which no other woman could ever satisfactorily compare. And when the connection is severed, and I have time to reflect on it, and whomev-*her*, the romanticist in me glorifies the relationship and the woman . . . especially if she has become stronger, less accessible and susceptible to my wiles (*i.e.*, more like Sarah).

I want whatever I do not have.

Does that make me a villain? A romantic? Or just plain pathetic?

Probably: none of the above. As long as free will is not leveraged by cash, coercion, or semi-automatic weapons, no *one* is to blame. Because:

• It takes two to tango;

And because the human impulse for sex, companionship, and connection is quick to be gratified and slow to accept reality, most of us humans probably remain in stale situations long past their expiration date.

Besides:

• The heart wants what it wants when it wants it.

Most of us, at various stages in our lives, have chosen mates:

• self-destructively;

• unwisely;

• neurotically;

• imperfectly.

The best we can expect from ourselves, when it comes to deciding on a mate for keeps, is to make the *least* self-destructive, unwise, neurotic, and imperfect choice.

Some of us, however, are so afraid of making the wrong decision that we make none. And we have no choice but to live with the consequences until and unless we're ready and able to change, or accept, them.

Alas, for a precious few, it may be too late.

You Can't Always Get What You Want (But if You Try Sometimes You Just Might Find You Get What You Need)

It is definitely too late for Connie and me. She is not interested in renewing any form of an interdependent romantic rapport with me; she doesn't even seem all that keen on keeping the communication lines open to repair our friendship.

She has had enough of my bullshit for one lifetime.

From: Sarah F
Sent: Monday 8:58 AM

I'm ba-a-a-ck. Happy new year! What did you do for the holidays?

Ah, yes, my old-new best buddy, returning home to determine if she and her husband could forge/salvage a civil union after nearly 25 years of slights, hurts, and scabs.

TWENTY-FIVE YEARS?

Stretch it out slowly, and it's still an eye's tick: T-w-w-w-e-e-e-n-n-n-t-y-y-y-f-i-i-i-i-i-i-i-i-i-v-e.

Say it fast or slow, it all comes down to the same: here today ... and gone ...

Tomorrow Is a Long Time

It gives one pause, enough to wonder:

- Has it really been 25 years?
- What if our engagement had lasted more than one night?
- Would *we* now be in counseling to repair our own frayed connection?

It would not be much of a stretch to conjure up that session.

Shrink: *How are you two this week?*

Me: *She won't let me play softball, poker, and basketball. She complains about Boys' Night Out and bingo night and book-club night and movie night ...*

She: *We have to talk ... this isn't working ... we're going to make a change ...*

Talk to Me

Wednesday 5:40 PM (one year after college graduation)

We were sitting on the loveseat in my basement apartment, perhaps two months after I'd moved in, having our regular mock-argument prior to my weekly poker game.

"You love poker more than me," she said.

You're right, Honey, I said. But only on Wednesday nights.

She aimed a lazy backhand at my forehead. I ducked. She sighed.

I kissed the base of her exposed neck before taking the southerly route, schussing past the supernal alps, lingering on each summit to savor the view, then heading down toward one of my favorite destinations in all the world, which—four years after my first visit—was still yielding hot spots of scenic and sensual pleasures.

"Not now," she whispered.

C'mon, baby, I whined.

"No pre-poker quickie," she said, followed by:

"We . . .

"Have . . .

"To . . .

"Talk."

Taken individually, each word has elemental, often powerful, meaning(s). But, when arranged in precise order, they become for most men the four most anxiety-inducing words in the English (and, I'm guessing, most every other) language.

Little good can come from such a pronouncement.

Perhaps the first time you hear this statement, you think (or may even say) one of the following:

- So start talking.

- *Have to*? I don't have to do anything I don't want to.

- What's with the formalities? You don't have to announce your intentions. Just spit 'em out.

But you were probably young at the time, a little impatient, maybe a tad cocky, and you likely got your ass handed to you . . . or the riot act read to you . . . or had sex withheld from you.

As you got older, you knew better. And you certainly knew that "We have to talk" was rarely followed with:

- about trading in the Jeep for the red convertible.

- about getting you that new home entertainment unit.

- about that threesome.

In most human intercourse, "We have to talk" is a prelude to:

- We found a tumor in your colon; it looks malignant.

- I want a divorce.

- We're going to make a change at second base.

In my experience with Sarah, the "we-have-to-talk" news was invariably bad, usually some variation of her break-up repertoire:

- I'm not happy.

- I'd like to see other people.

- I've been seeing other people.

However, on that distant evening, the sharp, lowdown, profoundly wounding pain in my gut that usually resulted from such a conversation starter was not present. She seemed to be serious about staying around for the long term. Maybe a little too serious.

"We have to talk," she repeated, and I found myself with a different feeling—a bilious, possibly pre-ulcerous nausea rising up from the bowels (figuratively speaking) of my abdominal cavity into the upper, frontal recesses of my brain. (Translation: my stomach and head ached.)

Ah, yes, *the* "commitment" discussion: a ten-minute opening act with the standard patter ("We're not getting any younger. . . . We've invested a lot of time and effort in this relationship. . . . Sometimes you just have to hold your nose and jump in") before the headliner made its appearance:

And here's . . . M-M-M . . . !

When all was said and done, every relationship came down to the M word. I had trouble saying it (but I could always type it with ease): Marriage.

Marriage.

Marriage.

Marriage.

It is a topic that chaperones you from first date to last. It is the subtext of all conversations. It is a constant intrusion to an inevitable conclusion.

Sarah and I had been together (again) for several months. We had jobs. I even had my own apartment. And she kept popping the same question: When? When? When?

Soon, soon, soon, I said.

I wasn't stringing her along. Not much. Not consciously. I wasn't ready. I needed more time—to think, to plan, to decide.

I knew then, and I know even better now, that my time would soon be up.

On that evening, sensing that I was already priming my poker face, she tossed out a new pitch, a slow curve—a nasty, knee-freezing yakker—that caught me looking.

"I want a baby," she said.

That shook me to attention.

Wha-a-?!? I wailed. Had I had all of my wits about me, I might've countered with a snappy: "Don't you already have one?" (Uh, that would be me.)

"I want a commitment from you," she continued, trying to reason with me. "A life together, a family."

Oh, jeez, please. Couldn't we just go back to our marriage discussion?

I told you she was smart: She had me nearly begging to discuss the forbidden topic.

"One more thing," she said. "If you won't pump some life into these shrinking ovaries, I'll find someone who will."

There it was, the ultimate ultimatum, the most threatening of all threats: abandonment. After all, I knew she could make good on it; she'd already proved it on several occasions, and sometimes when there was no occasion at all. (A line that good should be repeated.)

Marry Me

You'd think all this talk of commitment and kids would've dampened my sexual ardor. But, as I mentioned, I was 23, and no conversational curveball yet mastered could dampen the wood I was swinging. Besides, I could be just as single-minded, persistent, and manipulative in pursuit of my own goals.

I knew, however, that I had to pull out something bigger and more solid than any cannonry previously deployed.

Okay, I said.

"Okay?" she said.

Let's do it.

"Uh-uh."

No, let's do the other thing. You and me. Together.

"You mean marriage?"

Yeah.

"Is that your proposal?"

Yeah.

"Do it again. For real."

I squatted down in my skivvies, readjusted my privates and took her hand in mine. I looked at her, the beautiful girl I'd been in love with since the moment I first spotted her across a crowded room. I could not imagine ever wanting someone more. I closed my eyes and made the biggest, broadest leap of faith any 23-year-old kid could possibly make.

Will you marry me? I asked.

I honestly don't remember if she answered me, or what she said. It may have had something to do with an engagement ring.

All I know is that, in principal, we both got we wanted.

Only problem: mine was over in minutes; while hers was just starting and, with luck, would last till death did us part.

The next morning, I was awash in moisture. The enormity of the sex-crazed vow had me tossing, pacing, turning, and sweating throughout the night.

At breakfast, I proposed another solution.

Honey, I said, I've been thinking.

"Yes, Hubby," she said.

In so many words, I broke off our unceremonious betrothal by arguing for a "more traditional, romantic engagement" to come.

When, when, when? She asked.

Soon, soon, soon, I said.

Someday Soon

From: Sarah F
Sent: Wednesday 11:17 AM

```
I think it's time that we got together. We
really should talk.
```

We
Really
Should
Talk.

Oh, goodie.

From: Lee S
Sent: Wednesday 1:41 PM

```
i can't wait.
```

The new year has rolled in, and I seem to be adequately coping with middle adulthood. I have found myself unusually productive (steadily working to finish a—*this*—book by its spring deadline); consistently joyful (in the company of my two nieces and two nephews); and even patiently sanguine (dutifully gathering the necessary receipts and resources to settle my annual due with the government . . . and, in the process, pay a visit to one of my oldest friends).

> **PAUL**, 6′1.5″, 238 lbs.; brown hair and eyes; has been a buddy of mine since we were 11, and my accountant for the last 23 years (nearly as long as he's been married to Arlene, a woman he met at summer camp). His adoptive mother died when he was nine; his adoptive father remarried a year later (several months before his sister was born to his second adoptive mom). Paul and I rarely see each other because he lives in the Westchester suburbs, and is happily overwhelmed with his immediate family. Within the past year, after his "mother" and "father" died, respectively, he began searching for his birth mother, as yet with no success.

"Not a very good year," Paul says, looking at my W-2 forms. "What are you working on now?"

I tell him.

"Yeah, I can relate," he says.

You can? To *the one that got away*? I am surprised, knowing that he'd met his wife at 15.

"We didn't date again till after college," he says, "and in between I had a few ex-girlfriends that I think about from time to time. But it seems to me that you're talking here about more than just lost love. It's the overall nature of 'loss,' no?"

Yes, I guess.

I am reminded of how much calamity Paul has endured; yet, as long as I've known him, he has never been one to complain.

How is it that some people expend little effort letting go, while others seemed ill- or unequipped to the same task? And why is there no apparent correlation between actual cataclysms abided and a commensurate concern with the nature, texture, and even appeal of dissolution and disaster?

We (as a species, individually and collectively) are just built differently—chemically, genetically, and spiritually.

Some people, like Paul, experience the early loss of a parent (while still trying to process the ordeal of adoption, and the integration of *another* mother's affections) with mathematical and philosophical equanimity. While others, like me, sail through youth without evident trauma, and yet cling to abandonment issues. (Even growing up, Paul was a grounded, if mischievous, kid, while I was a moody little s.o.b. in school, on playgrounds, and around the house.)

Our House

I grew up with two diametrically opposed viewpoints when it came to letting go . . . or not. My father, a Schreiber (which means *writer,* or *scribe,* in German)—whose people came here from Eastern Europe and Russia, constantly *kvetching* about time's cruel, quick passage—was constitutionally disposed to reminisce about his good old days, almost as if just being old made them good. He passed this trait on to me, and I've obviously nurtured it well past maturation.

My mother's people—originally named Hertan (*hartan* means *hunk of meat* in Romanian, which indicates they were likely butchers) and Zucker (means *sugar* in German, so they were probably bakers) who emigrated from the Old Countries under similar duress and distress—were a hardier breed: a business, not a creative, class; doers, not thinkers (definitely not dreamers); much less sensitive (arguably *insensitive*), but more adept at adaptation. With relative unanimity, they seemed to have a much easier time of it (life), and of letting go (death).

I've often wondered: Where did Dad's insecurities come from? D.N.A.? His poor neighborhood? A hypochondriacal mother? A sainted, yet distant, father?

By all accounts, my father, Julian, was a smart, handsome, funny, athletic kid—with three older sisters and a younger brother who adored his every colon disturbance—yet he had insurmountable difficulty appreciating and accepting his own gifts. He was a very talented artist, *scribing* with pens, pencils, and brushes outstanding images; he could have made a living as an illustrator or even a painter. Pursuing any further education, however, even with the G.I. Bill for currency, was not in the cards for a young man with shaky self-confidence and an almost canonical devotion to his family, especially an idealization—and idolization—of *his* dad, a quiet, kindly, polite, 5'3" milkman from Poland or Austria (so reticent was Grandpa Max about mentioning any personal details, no one was ever sure exactly where he came from) who left the house well before sunrise, worked till sunset, and slept the rest of every day except Sunday. To my father, it was never a question: he would serve his country with honor overseas; then he would come home to get a job and help out his family. Maybe someday, if there was time, he'd attend to his own needs. By the time I met him, he was a fully formed adult, nearly 30, whose days were spent pleasing other masters: my mother; his *schmatte* business partners; me.

A Father and a Son

I was definitely a daddy's boy. At birth I bypassed my mother's breast (not that it was ever offered) to hang with my dutiful, nostalgic, underdog-defending father. But the world of men had another side: depressive, incommunicative, and withholding. I spent most of *my* days clamoring for male approval that too rarely came my way.

I've long since forgiven my father (and his forefathers) for any inherited or acquired deficiencies in my own personality. However, there has been no doubt of his/their huge effect.

Cruel to Be Kind

I played on a number of team sports in junior high and high school, but Dad never came to watch. He had already stopped attending Little League games because, he said, it was too painful for him to watch me being so hard on myself. I interpreted that to mean: he was embarrassed by my actions.

Whatever his reasons, I just wished that he had taken me aside and talked to me, helped me try to figure out why I was so hard on myself, and why my self-image seemed to rise and fall with how well or how poorly I played on a particular day. Until his latter years (certainly his *last* year, when we finally exchanged gushy articulations of genuine affection), his unspoken message remained: "Don't draw attention to yourself. Keep your head down and do your job. If you're looking for praise, look elsewhere."

The following incident hammered home this pivotal lesson:

I was maybe eight or nine, thrilled to be participating in a rare father-son football game—four kids and four adults intermingled in two teams—on the street where we lived.

The boys thought it was neat and funny to see our old men try to stretch and strut their stuff. (Who knew Strauss's dad was such a spaz?) And the fathers got a kick out of seeing their kids, eager to impress, run such tight, disciplined patterns.

The score was tied. Back in the huddle I told my father, our QB, that I could definitely beat Bobby Epstein on a fly route. Dad told me to can the braggadocio and, not wanting to favor his kid, called Strauss's number instead.

After the snap, Strauss fell down—this was after all, unpaved gravel we were playing on—but my father didn't see and threw the ball into the end zone. I got on my horse (as Coach White used to say) and hauled ass past Bobby Epstein and everyone else to tap the bulleted spiral softly into the air with a few outstretched fingers and then haul it into pay dirt by grabbing it with both hands. It *was* an amazing catch.

"Oh, yeah, baby. I am the man!" I taunted (or what was then the nine-year-old equivalent). I was celebratin' and showboatin' and stickin' the ball in Epstein's face when whoomph! The palm of Dad's hand whacked the back of my head. "What the—!"

My father had hit me maybe three times in my life, and this was the only time he ever did it in public.

"Don't you ever pull that crap again!" he seethed. "Just catch the ball, and keep your mouth shut. And no fuckin' hotdogging."

I'd also never heard him curse in public before.

That was the last father-son football game we ever played.

As I've said, my father was an extremely kind and sensitive man. I know that he *really* did feel worse than me after this incident. But he never mentioned it, nor did I.

Who knows how this incident affected me. Who

knows how, or if, my father's self-esteem issues became mine. Who knows how much happier my father might've been if he could have verbalized some of his childhood traumas. Whether he inherited this belief, observed it at home, or experienced it in the war, he maintained to his dying day that if you called attention to yourself, if you raised your head above the crowd, it was that much more likely to get shot off.

No use bemoaning or begroaning about it. That's just the way it was (or the way we were), and sometimes you just have to accept it and move on.

Mother and Child Reunion

What of my father's wife (my Ma)? What had the self-entitled-to-the-good-things-in-life, gusto-grabbing Queen of Darkness bestowed on me?

Conventional wisdom has usually equated the so-called negative traits—assertiveness, competitiveness, and self-absorption—as the lioness's share of my matriarchal inheritance. Yet, whenever friends and foes perceive or define me so baldly as my mother's son, I am invariably surprised. Shouldn't they know me better? Wasn't that obstinate, controlling, hard-case persona just something that I invented as a young, self-protective adult? Wasn't my true nature characterized more solidly as creative, compassionate, and empathic (more like my dad)?

An enlightened society encourages its kids to be kids, and

not be so quickly branded or demarcated by, say, superficially descriptive attributes, features, habits, mannerisms, qualities, quirks, and traits. Perhaps parents themselves should not, likewise, be as neatly and facilely categorized. It was probably unfair to both Mom and Dad to hold on to age-old beliefs and perceptions about their respective natures (and mine). We did the best we could with the tools we had.

Circumstances, however, dictated a much more thorough investigation into *both* sides of my ancestral legacy to discover what—and who—I am really made of.

11

Inarticulate Speech of the Heart

Mama Said There'd Be Days Like This

My mother was on the phone.

"Lee," Ma said (a rare formal address, so I knew it was something serious), "I'm here in the hospital. Your father isn't feeling too well."

And so it began, at noon, a round of phone calls that would end two hours later with my mother's soul-piercing scream, a sound I would never trivialize by trying to duplicate.

It meant, of course: "Your father is dead."

It doesn't matter how old the offspring, nine or 90, a parent's passing will fundamentally change that child. One of the few people you could count on, in crisis or calm, who had your well-being and welfare at the uppermost of his concerns, who had your back, day after day after day, had reached the end of his days. You were that much more alone in the world, that much closer to—and lonelier in facing—your own demise.

I immediately discovered that I was infinitely more capable of dealing with imaginary, symbolic cataclysm than with the real flesh-and-blood kind. As the eldest child, however, I had an example to set. I was the man of the house now. There were two younger siblings, their two spouses and four offspring—and of course our mother—who needed to rely on someone with a clear head and a strong shoulder. And so, I kept my grief well contained for 36 hours, until midnight before the 11 AM funeral.

Me and My Shadow

Earlier in the day I'd been playing catch with my youngest nephew (and godson), Zachary, then nearly five, a smart, funny bundle of energy, affection, and surprising sensitivity. If the two of us are in the same room, we're inseparable—you need a crowbar to pry him loose from me (we both hate to let go). For some reason, long since passed from a toddler's memory (maybe he got it from watching the Golf Channel with his grandfather), Zach has called me "Chi-Chi" (rhymes with *wee-wee*).

"Chi-Chi," he said, tossing a softball-sized rubber ball to me on the front lawn of his suburban home.

Yeah.

"Do you think Bahbee's in heaven?" (Years ago, my other beloved nephew-godson, Alex, now 13, came up with Bahbee—accent on the *bah*—maybe as some hybrid of Bubbie and Bob, neither of which was my father's name.)

I guess, I said.

"Throw it up to the sky," Zach said. "Throw the ball, Chi-Chi."

I threw the ball pretty high, and it rattled around the tree before bouncing back onto the lawn.

"Bahbee dropped it," he said, enjoying his joke so much that he fell on the ground laughing.

I looked over at Ma, who was lying on a chaise lounge with her eyes closed, but she seemed to be suppressing a small smile.

"Again, Chi-Chi!" Zach ordered.

I threw it again, and again it came back down.

"Again" and "again," the little tyrant directed me. And again and again, he'd say: "Bahbee missed another one . . . Bahbee missed another one . . . "

I was getting a little tired of this pastime. Also: the little brat was, in effect, disrespecting my father's fielding skills.

Uh, earth to mope: Get over it. The kid's having fun. What kind of man did your father raise? So I threw the ball softly into the tree, and it landed right in the cradle of two branches, like an egg in a nest.

"Bahbee caught it! Bahbee caught one!" he yelled, running inside the house to tell his father, my little brother.

My mother and I both got a pretty good smile out of that.

Round Midnight

At around 11 PM, with Zach on the floor of his room in a sleeping bag and me in his "big-boy" bed, he again engaged me in theological discourse:

"Chi-Chi?"

Yeah.

"Do you think Bahbee's in heaven?"

What do you think?

"I think he is."

Then he is.

"Chi-Chi?"

Yeah.

"If he's not, do you know anyone else in heaven?"

I guess. Why?

"To get my ball back."

Smart, funny kid. You had to laugh.

Now, get to sleep, I said.

Three seconds later, the kid was out. My night was just beginning.

Not Supposed to Break Down

I was later told by the adults in the family that my cater-wauling was heard throughout the house, upstairs and down.

So, sue me.

It must have lasted, off and on, for about 15 or 20 minutes when I was startled in mid-sob by a warm hand on my arm.

"Are you okay?" Marion, my mother, said.

> **MARION,** 72, once 5'5" (now 5'3"), 127 lbs.; once brown-haired (now "unknown"); green-eyed; retired insurance broker; married the love of her life when she was barely past 20, only to "lose" him, as she says, 50 years later. Ma, I respond, he's not lost, only momentarily misplaced. As a young mother, she was admittedly short on the "nurturing" part: "I couldn't wait till you kids grew up." As a grandmother, however, she's shown heretofore unseen/unheard patience, understanding, and kindness.

"Let's talk," she said to me.

It was the two-word variation of "We Have to Talk," "Do You Have a Minute," and "Come into My Office" that so filled many men (in particular) with anxiety and annoyance.

"Little good can come of it," my father used to say. Left unspoken was the idea that *it* (discussing stuff) was unmanly. To express one's inner self was a childish or, worse, feminine pursuit.

Years of relationships, therapy, and unclehood somewhat softened my viewpoint (which is exactly the point, some men would still argue). Besides, on that night, I was relieved to share the load.

My mother could, and can, talk about anything, anytime. Two vodka gimlets (no more, no less) at sunset and she's especially good to go on any subject. Except one.

There was a single topic she deemed *verboten,* though none of us knew about it until 14 years ago, coinciding with my sister's pregnancy. Ma sat us all down and said there was something she wanted to tell us, a secret "that I've kept from all of you," including her husband, "for so many, many years."

What could it be? My first thought: She gave up a baby for adoption.

"When I was ten," Ma said, "my mother was sent away to an asylum for six months. She was diagnosed with some form of depression, and had several shock treatments." And then my mother broke down in uncharacteristic sobs, apologizing to all of us, especially my father, who was stroking her arm and neck in an equally uncharacteristic display of public affection.

That's it, Ma?

We tried to ease her pain the best we could—mostly by keeping it light and jocular.

"I always thought Grandma was a little crazy," my

brother said, "especially when we found her 'washing' the lettuce with soap detergent."

"Or," my sister added, "when we found a plastic bag filled with what we thought were mice turds, and then discovered they were chocolate chips that she spit out because the chips were too hard on her false teeth."

"Why didn't she just buy *plain* ice cream?" my sister-in-law asked.

'Cause it wasn't on sale that week, I said.

"And I thought the secret was that *all* of our kids were adopted," my father said.

My mother forced a smile. "Thanks," she said to us. "I feel better after finally getting that out of my system."

We said: "The least we could do. No big freakin' deal. Nothing to gain by dredging up anymore."

However, it was freakin' big—it explained volumes about our mother's compulsion to control everything and everyone—and *we* (the rest of the family) did have trouble dealing with Ma's vulnerability. We wanted her to reassume her role as tough, stoic queenpin—the hard, dependable center of this family—so we could return to ours.

That single "event" formed the core of my mother's character, and *her* persona. That she had been able to repress the memory and progress greatly as a wife, mother, and businesswoman were efforts worthy of a Dickensian heroine. But these were neither the best nor worst of times, and none of us felt the need for any further examination.

When it was suggested that perhaps *she* should talk to a professional in depth about this incident and its aftermath, my mother—who throughout her life believed in and often submitted her children to, the mental health process—had this to say in response: "I don't want to find what's buried there."

The Kind of Love
You Never Recover From (Reprise)

In the funereal tradition of his forbearers, we sent my old man (his spirit? soul? old bones?) off on a journey none of us had ever taken. My brother's eulogy was eloquent and funny. My sister was solemn and touching. I was a honking, choking mess. But we all got through it, humbled and touched and melancholic beyond words, but probably feeling better for being able to share the essence of old "da" with the immediate world.

I became *indubitably* (one of my father's favorite words) a better man for having stayed up there, laboring to reach an audience that struggled to hear and cringed to observe.

These were no run-of-the-mill last rites. Our zeal, verbiage, and bathos surpassed send-offs for heroic philosopher-kings. (Why is it that the passing of public men, no matter how respected, leads to more spectacle and speechifying than the simple expression of genuine, personal grief for *seemingly* unremarkable men who were assuredly more *loved*?).

To his children, of course, my father was heroic—for a thousand different banal, unremarkable reasons (one of my favorites: if we mentioned at dinner some small item that we needed—a three-ring binder and a jockstrap come to mind—he'd walk in the next day and wordlessly hand us the thing we barely remembered even discussing). And none of those reasons or anecdotes was concocted or embellished by us merely because he was gone. We *always* felt that way. Absence did not make our hearts grow any fonder; it only damaged them irreparably.

Our father, a private man who had difficulty acknowledging his own worth, would have been plenty pissed and embarrassed at our excessive display. But he would have been damned proud, too.

A Hard Day's Night

The night before my dad's funeral, I should've been the one consoling my mother.

"I can't imagine how you must be feeling," I said (when I finally composed myself enough to speak). And then, in a remark so telling that it could only been borne out of such anguish: "This must be the reason why I never married. I would not have been able to cope with a loss of this magnitude."

My mother squeezed my hand.

"I'm not sure if I'll be able to," she said.

Six months later, to the consternation and surprise of her three children, my mother had a boyfriend.

"A day doesn't go by that I don't miss your father," she said. "But I discovered that I just wasn't nearly as tough and independent as I thought I was. Being alone was just too difficult."

Who knew?

Simple Twist of Fate

Sarah and I schedule a second "date" for us to get together again and, presumably, talk. Bill says he has no objection as long as it's for brunch.

Saturday, 1:11 PM

"Do you believe in fate?" she asks me as soon as we are comfortably seated.

Not really.

"I definitely believe that things happen for a reason," she says. "I don't think it was an accident that you contacted me at this time in my life."

You can always find meaning if you look for it, I say. Sometimes, shit just happens.

"I envy your clarity," she says.

Huh? Is that sarcasm? Are you talking to *me*?

"Well, you seem to be farther along in the process," she says. "I'm still flailing about in disarray and chaos, while you clarified what should have been our position from the outset."

Okay.

"I'm still a little unclear."

How so?

"When you wrote that you're taking yourself 'out of the romantic equation'—which, in my editorial opinion, sounds clunky and forced—were you giving me an advance peek at the book's ending?"

First off, I say: You're right. The "romantic equation" line is clunky, but we're stuck with it now. Secondly: I'm not sure I understand your question.

"Is this your non-fictional account of the future?"

I'm not sure what the future holds, so I can only surmise. If you're asking me if I'm removing the romantic equation now (in real life), but waiting until the finale to write it into the book, I would say: No. In a non-fictional account like this one, the essential details must be absolutely true—in spirit, if not in every actual fact. If you're asking me for a clue to the finale, I don't have one. And even if I did, I wouldn't say. We're both going to have to wait until the facts are in—and the choices are made—on the day all of the copy is due. [I don't imagine *that* is very clear to anyone.]

"It must be confusing for you."

What do you mean?

"Writing about your life as you're living it."

Oh, yeah. Everything is happening in real time, so it's a bit disorienting (mostly, in a good way). Sometimes, though, I wonder if I'm not making decisions based on what will make a stronger narrative.

"Okay, then, what's your best-case conclusion?"

Too soon to tell.

"Come on, it's just us—a couple of old friends chatting," she says. "What would you *like* to happen?"

I try to ignore her questioning.

"Well?"

I try to ignore her badgering.

"I'm not gonna stop badgering you until you tell me."

Fuck you.

"Okay, good. *Now* we're clear."

No, no, no, th-th-at's not what I meant . . .

As Time Goes By

The waitress halts my stammering and phumphering (another favorite word of Dad's) with the arrival of our omelettes.

"Hot plates," she says. "Be careful."

We chew a while on our respective dishes.

Sarah breaks the silence: "I guess I never foresaw our becoming reconnected as something that would lead to loss. But, regardless of what happens from here on, it seems like there will be loss on some front."

Good eggs, I think.

"Even when we think we can control things," she continues, "our uncontrollable emotions take charge, and loss is beyond our ability to anticipate or prevent."

Amen, sister. By the way, I ask her, how're things in counseling?

"Which one?" she asks.

Individual.

"You've very much been a part of my discussions with my shrink," she says. "She sees you as bringing joyful things back into my life."

I turn to look behind me. Surely, she must be talking to, and about, someone else. Certainly few ex-girlfriends ever expressed the belief that I could be a vehicle for anything other than criticism and torment. Only with my nephews and nieces could I ever be called a messenger of unconditional love and joy. But here, again, Sarah finds the positive, sunnier side to accentuate.

"I've often said to Laura [her shrink]," Sarah says, "how much I've enjoyed just doing some of the simple things with you."

That's nice to hear, I say. Polishing off the last morsel on my plate, I ask: Would you like to take a walk after lunch?

"That's just what I'm talking about," she says. "I love to walk; I can walk for hours. But Bill can't be bothered."

Again: how strange that I keep coming out on the long end of these comparisons. But: You're being unfair, I say to Sarah. You can choose any nitpicky trait about a person and cite it as greater proof of one negative thing or another. After being with someone for so long (I can only imagine), there are bound to be a few things that bug you. Besides, I'm not sure if you know me well enough now to begin ennobling any of my assumed traits or qualities. And I would caution you not to hold me up as an exemplar of *anything*, especially if you're using it (me) to throw in Bill's face during an argument or a therapy session. That's exactly why I should not be lurking around with any possible romantic intent. A wise man in a movie (*Casablanca*) once said: "The problems of two people don't amount to a hill of beans in this crazy world."

"You've always wanted to say that, haven't you?" Sarah says. "The next thing you'll be telling me: 'This could be the start of a beautiful friendship.'"

Well it is. Isn't it?

12

The Other Side of This Life

Changes in Latitudes, Changes in Attitudes

Saturday, 2:52 PM

We don't have all day. Sarah promised to be home by 7 PM. It is, after all, Valentine's Day (a fact that I probably should've noted sooner). We do have a few more hours, which we spend talking—and walking—along the water (the Hudson River) on Manhattan's west side.

How are the couples' sessions going? I ask her.

"I suppose pretty well," Sarah says. "It took a little while to adjust to another therapist's style. But she's very good, too. She doesn't let us stray much, listens well, remembers what we've said in prior weeks, and has no problem calling us to task without seeming biased. I can't say, however, that I'm too optimistic about the whole process."

Why not?

"I'm not sure if either one of us can fundamentally change. And, if so, for how long? I don't know if a few months of counseling can prevent the lava from destroying the village. I think the volcano will probably always be there, dormant and waiting to erupt. How's that for a dramatic analogy?"

Not bad. What are the main issues?

"Bill says I took out my anger on him for the first 20 years or so of our marriage," she says, "and that he accepted it like a dutiful husband. Now, he believes it's his turn. He wants me to give him the space and freedom to express his anger without me responding in kind. Basically, he wants to vent until he gets it out of his system."

I think we'd all like a piece of *that* therapy, I say. What about you? What do you want?

"I want him to empathize with me on my own terms, not his," she says. "And I don't want him to 'fix' things, just to listen when I vent."

Ah, yes, one of the basic differences between a man and a woman.

"Why is that?"

Beats me.

"The shrink has asked us to practice the art of 'intentional dialogue' outside of therapy."

What's that?

"Beats me," she says. "It's mostly just talking and listening. Unfortunately, we spend most of our time arguing about the rules of 'intentional dialogue.' I guess a lot of it comes down to our respective 'control' issues."

But what *is* intentional dialogue? I've never heard of that.

"Part of its purpose, I think," Sarah says, "is to return us to a primal childhood state, whereby 'Sarah' is again the little girl scolded and controlled by her father, and 'Bill' is the young son of parents who don't accept him."

Sounds like big fun.

Papa Don't Take No Mess

"Ironically," she says, "this has led to me to talk—in individual therapy— about the many similarities between my father and you."

You as in *me*?

"Yes. You're both insufferably independent, stubborn, intellectual elitists (though my father gave more weight to education) and loners; liberal (in the old-fashioned meaning); honest to a fault; passionate, intense, moody, petulant, and high-strung; unwilling to compromise; idealistic (though both of you use cynicism as a cover)."

Sounds about right. Any differences?

"My father made more compromises, and suffered for them," she says. "My father was probably more unforgiving and unable to back down. My father was not as communicative as you. My father was bald and you're not—as yet."

I can live with those comparisons, too.

"Your turn," she says. We'd often joked how similar Sarah was to my mother.

Synchronicity

Okay, I'll play: You're both Virgos, whatever that means. There're some physical similarities ("young" photos of my mother bear a great resemblance to Sarah). You both appear to be very tough and independent, but you're really a couple of softies. If crossed, you and Ma can be very cold and withholding. You two are very loath to give up grudges. Also, you each tend to see things overwhelmingly from your own perspective (even though you keep nodding as if you completely understand the other person's viewpoint). You're both pragmatic, as opposed to sentimental (but maybe that's another man-woman difference). Neither one of you has much patience for crybabies. Your first instinct is to blame others for your mistakes; perfectionism and control are major issues. You both love to travel. Perhaps one of the most significant similarities is how you two have mellowed with age, certainly as it relates to me: You both used to be quite stingy with the compliments, whereas now you're my biggest fans (I'm paraphrasing).

"Fair enough," she says.

Saturday, 5:49 PM

It's a good day, another fine time spent in each other's company. We've caught up on most of the outstanding particulars in our lives, leaving only one last item to catch: a train.

"Do you have anything I can read on my ride home?"

I've finished today's *Times*.

"I was thinking of something more original." Observing my uncomprehending expression, she adds: "From the book."

Oh. No, I don't happen to have a few hundred manuscript pages in my back pocket.

"I thought you might have some new material ready for me to look over," she says.

Not yet.

"When?"

Soon.

"When?" she repeats.

Tomorrow, I say.

From: Lee S
Sent: Sunday 11:52 AM

enclosed: the first 150 (approximately) pages of
the manuscript. you're the first person to read
this material, so i'm eager to hear your
response.

I don't hear from her for almost four entire days, which is
quite unusual. Other than a couple of breaks over the past six
months—when either of us was out of town or computer
inaccessible—this is the longest period she's gone without
writing me.

I send another shout-out.

From: Lee S
Sent: Thursday 10:24 AM

is anyone out there? are you talking? are you
reading?

Things We Said Today

From: Sarah F
Sent: Thursday 4:19 PM

I read through the manuscript last weekend, and
ever since I've been trying to sort out my
conflicted feelings. I wasn't too thrilled with
seeing my e-mails so thoroughly documented.
While you indicated that you would be using

this material, I'm surprised to see them as
such a large part of an ongoing thread. Also,
some of the sexually charged descriptions made
me a little uncomfortable.
Mostly, though, it's been Bill's negative
reaction to the idea of a book (no, he hasn't
read anything yet) that has been so disturbing
to me. As was the opinion expressed by our
therapist in couples counseling. Basically, she
wanted to know, Why and how I could allow this
to occur? Couldn't I see, she said, how self-
destructive and potentially damaging to my
family this material could be?
Right now I feel like the bad guy all around.
Some of it is guilt (which Bill has been
feeding) for sharing so many intimate details
with you . . . and for allowing them to be
chronicled so openly. I feel especially
defensive trying to explain to him how our (his
and mine) relationship has been in a bad place
for a long time, and you being there to listen
(as a friend) has been a great help to me.
I'll try to write again soon when I have a
better handle on the situation . . .

My response is sympathetic and concilatory, reiterating my
concern for her, and her family.

From: Sarah F
Sent: Friday 10:52 AM

I told you from the start that I didn't want
anyone to get hurt in this [book] process, and

for the most part I can live with what you've
written thus far. But, as the reality sets in,
and I can envision this stuff being published,
I am becoming increasingly anxious. I'm not
sure that Bill is going to be too thrilled when
he reads this material. And I've only just
begun to think about the ramifications for my
children. My daughter, in particular, could be
quite upset reading about her parents' troubles
and foibles.
I guess I would expect that you wouldn't put
anything into print that you wouldn't want to
see written about your nephews, nieces, sister,
brother (and in-laws) and mother.

Again, I try to soothe and mollify.

From: Sarah F
Sent: Monday 9:04 AM

This weekend was pretty rough. I am afraid that
Bill is suffering more than I'd thought from
our (your and my) relationship, and that has
disturbed me more than I'd imagined. I do know
I am not prepared to end my marriage. I think
there is one concrete thing that I have learned
about myself over the past several months: I'm
not ready to be on my own. Maybe life and
relationships are more about compromise and
adaptation than I've cared to believe. Maybe
it's time for me to grow up a little more.
There isn't much more to say at this point
because Bill and I need to talk things through.

You see what is going on here? I am being manipulated by both of them in their battle for control. Depending on your choice of metaphor, it seems that I have become a:

- ▸ wedge
- ♟ pawn
- © bargaining chip
- ✸ smokescreen.

The writing is on the wall, and it seems to me that I am about to get:

- 🔩 screwed.

From: Sarah F
Sent: Wednesday 9:19 AM

For several months, your presence in my life has fulfilled a dual purpose: it has fueled my resistance to making changes in my relationship with Bill; and it has provided a sounding board for much of the internal strife with which I have been suffering. The depth of that relationship is preventing both Bill and me from truly addressing the myriad of problems that were there for many years.
It has become increasingly evident that Bill is citing us (you and me) as one of the main problems threatening our marriage. Whether or not he's right, I do feel that it is a factor preventing me from determining objectively whether or not my marriage is redeemable.
I don't know what this means for me or for Bill, or for you for that matter. I'm just

trying to work it all out without too much pain for anyone, but it seems evident that some changes, and hard choices, must be made.

Can you believe I was so naïve that I didn't see it coming? (Did you? Did you expect she'd ditch me at the first sign of real trouble?) Could you believe that I'd again be taken in by her apparent openness of heart and mind? Could you believe that after all this time she still had the capacity to hurt me?

Believe it.

And, in response, I e-mail her the following screed:

From: Lee S
Sent: Wednesday 5:25 PM

SINCE OUR REUNION DINNER, NEARLY EIGHT MONTHS AGO, I THOUGHT WE HAVE BOTH BEEN ON THE SAME:

📄 PAGE.
〜 WAVELENGTH.
🌍 PLANET.

BUT, AT THE FIRST SIGN OF TROUBLE, YOU SHUT DOWN AND HIGHTAIL IT. AND—THIS MAY BE THE MOST INFURIATING ASPECT OF IT ALL—YOU USE AS YOUR RATIONALES MANY OF THE EXACT SAME THINGS I'VE BEEN SAYING TO YOU FOR MONTHS. SUCH AS: WORK ON YOUR MARRIAGE; FIX THE PROBLEMS AT HOME; DON'T COUNT ME IN A "WHAT-IF" SCENARIO . . .
I DON'T ESPECIALLY CARE THAT YOU'RE PASSING OFF MY THOUGHTS AS YOUR OWN, ONLY SO FAR AS I THINK YOU'RE MANIPULATING THEM FOR YOUR BENEFIT, AND TO MY DETRIMENT. BOY, IS *THAT* A FAMILIAR FEELING. WHEN I FIRST CONTACTED YOU, I

COULD NOT HAVE ANTICIPATED THE LEVELS OF
SIMPATICO, UNDERSTANDING AND INTIMACY THAT WE'D
REESTABLISH IN SUCH A RELATIVELY BRIEF TIME.
WHICH IS WHY I'M SURPRISED AND DISAPPOINTED
THAT YOU'D SO SOON ABANDON THE INTEGRITY OF OUR
FRIENDSHIP WITHOUT EVEN A DISCUSSION . . .
IF YOU WERE HAVING SECOND THOUGHTS ABOUT OUR
RELATIONSHIP, YOU OWED ME THE COURTESY OF A FULL
AND DIRECT EXPLANATION. INSTEAD I RECEIVED
VIRTUALLY NONE AT ALL. YOU LEFT IT TO ME TO
READ BETWEEN THE LINES (JUST LIKE I HAD TO DO
WHEN WE WERE YOUNGER). I AM AWARE OF HOW MUCH
MY PRESENCE HAS EXACERBATED YOUR TENSION AND
CONFUSION AT HOME, AND I'LL TAKE DUE
RESPONSIBILITY FOR THAT. BUT I DON'T THINK IT'S
FAIR TO HANG THE CRUX OF YOUR PROBLEMS ON ME;
YOUR MARITAL DIFFICULTIES PRECEDED MY ARRIVAL BY
MANY YEARS. BESIDES, I'VE DONE LITTLE BUT
ENCOURAGE YOU TO FIX YOUR DISTORTED THOUGHT
PROCESSES AND SELF-DESTRUCTIVE BEHAVIOR. BY YOUR
OWN ADMISSION, MY SUGGESTION LED YOU INTO
THERAPY. YET, FOR SOME REASON, I BELIEVE YOU
CHOSE TO CONCEAL THAT CRUCIAL PIECE OF
INFORMATION FROM BILL. HOW COME? SO YOU COULD
DEPLOY IT WHEN IT MOST FITS YOUR PURPOSE? AM I
COMPLETELY OVERREACTING, OR DID YOU BEHAVE LIKE
A FOUR-FLUSHING WEASEL? JUST ASKING.

I Have Finally Come to Realize

Boy, do I go off on her, ranting in ALL CAPS, not braking for a
single shift, while the anger pours out of me.

Where does this anger come from? Is it really all directed at her? Am I in any way justified? And, even if she did act in a weaselly manner, does it really warrant such a RELENTLESSLY HARSH AND LOUD response?

What is *really* bothering me? Did I half hope that, this time, she would not just follow my lead and *react*, but actively pursue a goal (like me) on her own? I would never have willingly been the catalyst to wreck her marriage, but what if she had been the one who, for a change, took the leap?

If I should have learned one thing on this journey, it is: Never immediately send off an angry letter or e-mail; sit on anything you write out of pique for at least 24 hours. A full day should be an adequate period in which to take some starch out of your collar, a little wind out of your sails, or even to burst the bile in your balloon. If, after rereading your words with a more lucid, calm, and objective eye, you still believe they're an accurate representation of your head and heart, by all means *send*.

That level of awareness and self-control, of course, has rarely stopped me before. I have always known in my head and heart that these irrational, impulsive, impetuous, impolitic outbursts *should* be contained (vented, perhaps, not released); however, this knowledge, had yet to be permanently imprinted into my P.O.V., D.N.A., or M.O. It is so much easier and more gratifying to trigger and discharge these base impulses. Explosions are *fun*: the big bang, the destruction, the fallout.

Besides, no man is an island until he burns all his bridges.

So why stop now?

Well, I don't exactly *stop*, cause I do send the letter. But I am, for the first time able to acknowledge almost immediately the impudence and imprudence of my words. I realize that *now* is the time to actually alter some of the behavior that, in retrospect, has proved to be clearly, incorrigibly, flat-out wrong.

Because Sarah really doesn't deserve the blunt, brunt end of my anger. Because she didn't say anything all that terrible. And because she does not have the capacity to hurt me as much as she once did.

Aging does have its benefits.

Besides: Who am I to lecture her on how to behave? It is the height of silly, self-serving *chutzpah* to think that I have the right to castigate, or lecture, her (or anyone else) for protecting her family. It must've been brain lock, temporary insanity, or (as my mother liked to blame when I behaved badly) "the gremlins" that allowed me to believe, for even a moment, otherwise. In addition: Don't I understand her well enough to know that she was just venting, that she'll soon be whistling a whole different tune?

For a change, I'm able to transcend my basic instinct *before* it's too late.

From: Lee S
Sent: Thursday 10:44 AM

```
i overreacted. i should not have sent that
ridiculous rant to
you until i had an opportunity to absorb and
process my feelings.
i was wrong, and i'm sorry.
would you feel better about this (book) process
if you could respond in your own words to "my"
story? we could set aside an entire chapter for
you to set the record straight on anything i've
written.
```

From: Sarah F
Sent: Thursday 11:11 AM

I accept your apology. I've heard (and said) a
lot worse over the years.
How long would my contribution have to be? When
would it be due?

From: Lee S
Sent: Thursday 2:17 PM

make your chapter as long as you like. the
deadline, as is most often the case in
publishing, was yesterday. or, failing that:
tomorrow.

Once you've got a taste for it, you can polish off an entire hum-
ble pie in a single sitting. I owe it to at least one other person to
try and digest another slice.

From: Lee S
To: Bill F
Sent: Friday 10:20 AM

hello, there. you've no doubt heard that i've
reentered the life of your wife (and,
indirectly, yours). i'm here to say that you
have nothing to worry about; my intentions are
purely chaste and honorable. it is only Sarah's
friendship that i desire, and perhaps yours as
well.
you've also been notified about my "book"

```
project. i thought it only fair that you should
read the material before it's published.
though it might not be immediately evident, i
have excised, trimmed and polished scads of
off-the-record, hugely embarrassing and
potentially-hurtful-to-your-family comments.
it is, however, only one man's opinion.
therefore, i'd like to give you the opportunity
to respond (with minimal editorial constraints
and absolutely no financial compensation) in
print. if you'd like, you can include an account
of your "one (or "ones") that got away."
i look forward to hearing from you soon.
```

In my diverse editorial career, I once worked part-time at the *New York Times* (on the sports desk as a copy editor). One reason my stint there was not more permanent, I've rationalized, is because of the paper's policy on headlines: no making sport (or punning) with proper names.

As a freelance author, of course, I have no such constraints. Therefore, I've entitled this section:

Bill of Goods

From: Bill F
Sent: Thursday 10:59 PM

```
I am, and have always been, aware that you were
one of the most important people in Sarah's
life. I'm sure we each have at least one of
those tucked away "lost loves" that have become
part of our fabric and can never be forgotten
```

or readily dismissed. I admit to my own
"ghosts," people that affected me dramatically,
and who I can never forget.

I have always respected the special
relationship you two had years ago and seem to
continue to have. And I like to believe I
understand it.
I also must say that, for whatever it's worth,
I have always liked you. I have told Sarah on
a couple of occasions that I could see what she
saw in you. Then again, her judgment is poor:
she settled for me.
I have always trusted, and will continue to
trust, my wife. I always figured that if you
can't trust the person you're with, you
shouldn't be with that person anyway. Besides,
I think Sarah will tell you that, by nature, I
am a very not-jealous person.
I may not be too thrilled about you writing
about me or my marriage, but I respect that you
were up front enough to contact me. That could
not have been an easy thing to do. And it has
to be difficult to open up your personal life,
in which I hear you're currently struggling, to
public scrutiny. I hope it works out for you.
I'd probably be open to writing a response to
your material. When can I read it? How long
should my contribution be? When is it due?
Hopefully, we can get together soon, maybe have
a couple of drinks, and talk about old times
and new.
All the best,
Bill

13

All She Wrote

> **SARAH** (married to Bill for 20-plus years, with two grown children), 5′5.5″, 128 lbs.; black (once brown) hair; brown eyes; nursery school director; finds herself in middle age with more questions than answers. Then, out of the blue, her college sweetheart swoops into her life, confusing some issues, clarifying others. She tries to do the right thing . . . for everyone.

What is the right thing?

What will become of them (she and the author)?

What will become of them (she and her husband)?

This is her chapter

"Chapter *thirteen*?" she says. "I didn't even know that books had a 13th chapter. I thought they skipped right to 14."

You're thinking of elevators.

"Whatever," she says. "Here's my contribution."

What I Did for Love

By Sarah F

Wow . . . quite a tale, huh?

I don't know all that much about the writing process, but I do have a few thoughts on the content of this story. The character, "Sarah," who is described in several instances as "smart," doesn't sound like the type of woman to falsely flatter her guy or intentionally lose to him in order to assuage his ego. So, how the hell does our author call this a non-fiction book and expect us to believe that he "usually won" when playing backgammon, checkers, chess, spades, poker, and Risk? My recollection of those contests is quite different, though the descriptions of poor sportsmanship are right on the money.

I guess my point is: I'd be feeling a lot more uneasy, and queasy, if I believed that *all* of this material was true. For arguments' sake, let's say *most* (certainly well above 75 percent) of what you've just read was factual. The next obvious question you might be asking me (as did I, my husband, my friends, and therapists): Why on earth did you so willingly participate in this endeavor? Are you:

- extremely loyal?

- extremely self-destructive?

- completely sadistic?

- completely narcissistic?

- really romantic?

- really pathetic?

- vying for sainthood?

- vying for martyrdom?

- flat-out nuts?

I suppose there's a little "all of the above" in my reasoning process. But I offer up another rationale in the form of this story.

Many, many, many (well, not *that* many) years ago, I fell madly, deeply in love with a boy and spent a portion of the next six years of my life growing up with him. The years we shared formed us as adults. The values, beliefs, and memories that grew out of those years became an integral part of my being.

I imagine it to be akin to imprinting (you know that study with the baby ducks) or like twins, forever connected in a bond that time and place can alter but never break. Love, in my vision, is a form of energy that is constantly changing form and shape but never disappears. The love you feel for your parents and children is always there, but do you love each one in the same way? Do you love your parents the same way you did when you were four and they were 40, or when you're 40 and they're . . . not? No need to answer. Then why should we expect romantic love to be any different? Why would we expect it to either remain constant or vanish into thin air? Surely, it doesn't. And I would challenge any of you in a long-term relationship to stare me in the face and deny that the feelings for the person who stole your heart at a dance or a club five, ten, 25, or 50 years ago remain as strong as when you first met. That love may change, but—if it was ever real—it will remain in your heart forever.

The heart really does have an endless capacity for love. If only we could keep it pumping endlessly and openly, and not let it wear down due to struggles with political correctness or social pressures. Wouldn't we all be far more happy, healthy, and at peace with ourselves if we could stay true to our hearts?

In many ways I suppose I could be described as foolish—

make that *reckless*—for my willingness to participate in this adventure. However, I (unlike our author) do believe in divine intervention. I believe there was a reason why he (the writer) contacted me at this time in my life, and I believe there was a purpose served by the subsequent chain of events. In the end, I had no real choice but to see it through. In other words: I feel that fate chose me.

Women *may* not be as sentimental as men, but we do have our moments. The simple, emotional truth of this matter is: What I did, I did for love . . .

For the love of my children: to free them from the conception that parents are any more or less than flesh, blood, heart, and mind; to help them learn that the true gift of love is forgiveness.

For the love of my husband: who, when our marriage needed work to save it, gave me his love and trust to explore many different avenues, knowing that all roads would eventually lead back home (despite his belief that a man and a woman can't be friends without the "sex thing" getting in the way).

For the love of an 18-year-old boy: whose soul will be forever connected to mine, and to whom I owed the opportunity to help heal his wounds.

For that boy who became a man: to help him in any (reasonable) way to tell his (our) story.

For a soul mate: who will always remain a dear, dear friend no matter how much time or distance passes between us.

And for all the ones you've loved and lost (and sometimes find again). They never really get away . . . do they?

Good stuff, huh? Especially from a nursery school director who has, in recent years, written little more than brochure copy and permission slips. I continue to applaud her candor, courage, and an unselfconscious facility for adept self-expression.

Though it's relatively late in the game, another new voice is about to enter the mix. He, too, seems to possess the requisite tools—equal parts passion, pain, and proficiency—to craft a brief, compelling narrative.

> **BILL,** 55, once divorced (now married to Sarah for 20-plus years, with two grown children); 5′10″, 193 lbs.; brown eyes; gray (once brown) hair; optician; says he thinks of himself as a "single guy." He still plays softball on summer Sundays, plays tennis on Wednesdays, and goes out for drinks with the boys on most Friday nights. He also characterizes himself as a "very not-jealous person" and a "frustrated writer."

Blinded by the Light
By Bill F

I was at a business function and knew most of the people there, but the room became spotlighted and framed with a single female figure centered in it; everything else was a soft, unfocused blur.

She stood up, and I took a photograph in my mind's eye: long, shoulder-length brown hair; a short but tasteful miniskirt, showcasing great legs in knee-high boots; poised posture and elegant gait. Behind large sunglasses, her bearing was regal and aloof, even a touch arrogant. If looks could talk, hers would've said: "I am better than you, and yet I am still a nice person."

Only when she was out the door did my surroundings come suddenly rushing back, visually and aurally, to reality. I thought, "Boy, would I like to sleep with that girl." All I knew of her was that her name was Roberta, and she was married.

At the time, I was 26 years old, single, and had never felt very committed to anyone. Sure, I had been married briefly once before, but that's another story suited for another book. I had begun to believe I was incapable of "love." Some switch or gene had not properly installed when I was born. Almost all the guys I knew were married with children. Presumably, they "loved" their wives. They knew something I didn't. Or they were in touch with their feelings and I wasn't. Or, perhaps, I had just set my standards higher than they did.

A year later, my mother passed away. Roberta came to my apartment to pay her respects. We talked at length for the first time, and got to know each other a little. A little was better than none at all.

Another month or two went by, and I heard that Roberta and her husband had separated. I made it a point to stop by her office, offering an empathetic shoulder to lean on and a helping hand, if needed. Was I sincere, or did I have an ulterior motive? Both, I'm sure.

Weeks later, I ran into her at my bank. I didn't even know that she lived in the same neighborhood. A conversation ensued, and I noted that she didn't appear to be in a hurry to go anywhere else. I took my shot: "Would you like to go to the beach tomorrow?" She immediately said, "Yes."

The next day went better than I could have possibly planned. For whatever reason, I had suddenly become the ideal date, something to which I could not have laid claim in any prior effort. I think I actually cared this time.

The day turned into the night, the night into the following

day, and before we knew it, she had moved in. But it was our first night together that still remains the most memorable. I learned something new: how to make love with my eyes open. I didn't want to miss a thing. I wanted to absorb, and remember, everything.

I still had commitment issues, however, and when she broached the subject of "love," I tried to change the topic. Later on, when the relationship became too much like work, I ended it. There were no hard feelings, and neither one of us looked back. Well, almost never. She had now become the standard by which I would judge every subsequent woman, and I resigned myself to the fact that I was destined to be single forever. Not having children troubled me a little, but I was otherwise satisfied. I was finally "okay" with myself.

About a year and five or six women later, some friends and I went out on a Friday night to go clubbing (we called it "disco-ing" back then). I walked in the door and glanced to my right. There stood Sarah. She was leaning against the bar, possessing a look as aloof and arrogant as I had ever seen. And yet, she seemed like she could be a nice person. I walked over to find out.

Very compelling work—by both of them. I couldn't have said their piece(s) any better myself. But I would have to try. I was contractually obligated to deliver another two chapters.

14

The End Has Begun

The end of all things is at hand.
—PETER 4:7

The world is round and the place [that] may seem like the end may also be the beginning.
—IVY BAKER PRIEST

Still ending, and beginning still.
—WILLIAM COWPER

This is not the end. It is not even the beginning of the end. But it is, perhaps, the end of the beginning.
—WINSTON CHURCHILL

Ends and beginnings—there are no such things. There are only middles.
—ROBERT FROST

Great is the art of beginning, but greater is the art of ending.
—LAZARUS LONG

Nothing ends nicely, that's why it ends.

—WINSTON CHURCHILL

*The future is the past, modified. So one's hope of the fu-
ture is still the past moving to what one considers to be
the future.*

   *The mind never moves out of the past. The future is
always the mind acting, living, thinking in the past. . . .
But one never ends anything completely and that non-
ending is one's hope.*

—KRISHNAMURTI

I reach a conclusion whenever I am tired of thinking.

—ANONYMOUS

Finally, in conclusion, let me say just this.

—PETER SELLERS

The End of My World Is Near

This won't be easy, writing and concluding these last two chapters, considering how much difficulty I have with letting go
and moving on.

   Let's start the completion process by going back to review
the questions posed earlier, and determine how we (I) did in
fully answering and explaining them:

☐ How often, if ever, did she (the one) think of me (and
in what context)?

☑ *Often (and in many different contexts).*

☐ Were my remembrances of our relationship accurate, or
had I been clinging to self-protective delusions?

☑ *A little of both, though considerably more accurate than delusional.*

☐ Could a man in love with his own youth find beauty in a woman who's no longer young?

☑ *Yes.*

☐ Was love blind, or just in need of a new prescription?

☑ *Yes.*

☐ Did this idealization of youth (and the perfect girl who accompanied it) permit or compel me to let go of other women in my past that I could've loved or perhaps did love?

☑ *Perhaps.*

☐ (If so, how could I track *them* down?)

☑ *Google. Match.com. Friendster.com. Reunion.com. Classmates.com. Lostlovers.com. Friends Reunited (in Britain). White Pages.*

☐ How did she—the up-till-now purported *one* truest love—respond to my intrusion into her life . . . with dismissive laughter, tears, annoyance, and/or a restraining order?

☑ *None of the above (though she may have teared up a bit).*

☐ Did I *not* marry her for the right reasons?

☑ *Mostly, yes.*

☐ Was she the one that got away?

☑ *In part, yes. But, for me, there were other missing people (my father) and missed opportunities (kids, possibly a wife) that had as much, or more, lasting impact.*

☐ Was I the one that got away from her?

☑ *Yes.*

☐ Was the idealization of youth (and the perfect girl who accompanied it) *the* thing that has prevented me from finding happiness with someone else?

☑ *Not <u>the</u> thing, but definitely one of many things.*

☐ Did I rekindle the flame of youth, or extinguish the torch I'd been carrying for so long?

☑ *Yes.*

☐ Were we soul mates?

☑ *For the most part, Yes. At least we were for the first half of our lives (see below).*

☐ Do I (or anybody else) get only one soul mate per life?

☑ *Probably, yes. Hopefully, no.*

☐ Can I (or anybody) live fully and happily without one?

☑ *Probably, yes. Hopefully, no.*

☐ If, for whatever the reasons, a person loses one soul mate, what are the odds that he or she (or I) will find another?

☑ *See below.*

Soul Mate

Sarah and I were soul mates, certainly during our six years together, and in my mind probably for another 15 years thereafter. Maybe more. Let's say we were soul mates for the first half of our lives. But now? Maybe, yes; maybe, no. But the point is moot since we won't be pursuing any agenda other than that of boon companions.

Had I made the move to contact her earlier, perhaps we would have acted more precipitously or rashly. To what end? We'll never know. We were so much younger then (we're so much older now). We're also a little smarter, and becoming—in spite of ourselves—more mature. What (or who) worked at age 24, or 34, does not work ten or 15 fifteen years later.

Let me tell you: *nothing* works the same.

As I make the turn and head toward the back nine, I'm going to need someone to help me tote that bag: another soul mate. And lots of luck.

What exactly are the odds?

Chances Are

For argument's sake, let's say the matchmaking gods have, somewhere in the world, sowed the seeds of at least one *additional* soul mate per soul on earth. Let's say that, in my opinion, most gods (even the Big Guy)—who often behave like glorified reality-show producers, manipulating our movements and emotions for their entertainment—have sprinkled cues and clues around the world for those of us who choose to play. And let's say it comes to my attention that there may exist a woman in, say, Sri Lanka who—on paper—is perfect for my silver and golden years. But let's say there are several obstacles in the way of our union, including at least *this* one: She lives (or did or will) in *fucking* (pardon my crassness) Sri Lanka!

Sri Lanka:

- an unlikely vacation destination, considering its unstable political situation;

- home to nearly 19.5 million Sri Lankans;

- a land mass of 25,332 square miles (slightly larger than West Virginia).

You do the math.

On the astronomical-to-one shot that I actually *meet* her (or her heirs or her parents), in Sri Jayewardenepura Kotte, the country's official capital, there's less than a 33-percent chance that she'll grasp the nuances of my charming patter (English is one of three national languages, along with Sinhala and Tamil).

Or, worse, what if she's a completely fluent *11* year old? I can't imagine the Sri Lankan government, or any other moderately civilized culture on earth, being too keen on having a middle-aged *gaijin* (or the Sinhalese equivalent) snatch away its choicest crop of homegrown young virgins. (And seducing virgins—much less pre-pubescent ones—is not a desire I remotely harbor.)

Or, perhaps, she's 82 (*and* a virgin), and I am just too shallow to see past her leathery wrinkles and hairy moles.

Or, most probably, she's already betrothed. In every subculture on the planet—except perhaps in the New York and Los Angeles metropolitan areas—nearly everyone, aged 25 to 50, is, has been, or will soon be (depending on the law in their state) married.

So, theoretically, even if there is another soul mate for me, chances are:

- We don't travel in the same circles.

- We don't live on the same continent.

- We don't speak the same language.
- She's married.
- She's below the age of consent.
- She's really, really old.
- She's dead.
- She hasn't been born yet.
- She hasn't been born yet (*and* she's engaged).

All things considered, the odds of me finding true love in the latter part of my life are roughly 53,478,092 to one, or about the same as losing to a straight flush with four aces (see below).

Everybody Wants to Rule the World

After Sarah broke up with me (the first time), I was one sorry sod. I was fragile, vulnerable, and—at age 19—entirely ill-equipped to deal with those emotions. I did what every other boy-man through the ages has done under the exact same circumstances: I concealed, denied, and reinvented.

To make sure that no speck of vulnerability or weakness would reveal itself, I created a new, improved persona: implacable, incommunicative, unreadable. In short: one sonovabitchin' poker player.

My inchoate feelings of rejection and melancholy were replaced by a sophomoric philosophy that included the essence of poker: master emotions, situations, and people; get to know them better than they know you.

I helped pay for college with money I made in local card games. Then I graduated to new stakes and new personnel, which eventually coalesced in something exceptional and wondrous: the Wednesday Night Poker Game.

Starting out at that card table were seven young men—all in our 20s, anxious and uncertain regarding the future. There, at the close of a work day, we would sit in cheap suits or our schoolyard best (T shirts, jeans, and sneakers), and scramble to be King of the Hill. Ace of the Whole. For several hours each week, we were ageless and timeless, excused from the constraints of adult behavior. We were, to a man, boys (with varying abilities to keep our childish rashness in check). The better we belied rash heat with surface cool, the better we fared in the Game.

For more than 15 years, the Game played on. It was our respite and refuge from jobs, families, relationships, and, for some, the ruins of splintered dreams. It was a constant in an unstable, unsettled universe. It was—for me, at least—where sweet victory far outpaced crushing ruin.

Until, one night, when everything seemed to change.

Against All Odds

Most mishaps in life are cumulative; they come unannounced and often go unrecognized. It's rare that you can cite a specific setback so profound that it overturns your essential belief system.

I won't belabor all of the details, just the major beats:

- In five-card draw, pot limit, I was dealt three aces. At the end of a progressive betting round, there remained three players in clockwise order: Lucky (short for Luckman, his real name), me, and Rich (also real).

- Lucky and I each drew one card (I was faking two pair); Rich drew two. The betting again got heavy until there was more than $1,000 on the table.

- Glancing at the huge pile of bills and chips, the biggest pot I'd ever been involved in, Lucky simply said: "Pot" (as in: I'm betting the entire amount in there).

- Whoa! Oy! Yep, even though I'd pulled the case ace—that's right, the one card I drew was the fourth bullet—I was not entirely elated. I'd played with Lucky for so long, and I knew him so well: this was no bluff; he had the goods. He couldn't have a Royal Flush (I had all the aces), so I was counting on him having maybe four ladies (Queens). Still and all, with a virtual lock of four aces, I was not confident enough to raise. I just called; Rich folded.

- I turned over my cards and said: Lucky, there's only one hand in the deck that beats me.

- He beat me with a straight flush to the Jack.

You know how rare it is to get four aces in 52-card draw poker? Or even rarer, to draw a straight flush? Can you imagine the odds of *both* occurring in the same hand? Nearly incalculable. I'm only guessing here, but I'd say they were 53,478,092 to one.

You've heard of the expression, Lucky in love, unlucky in cards? I figured if I quit playing poker for a while, I might be able to improve my chances of finding true love in middle age.

It Once Was My Life

So, how are you coming with an ending for the book? asks my friend Phil.

If you recall, before I'd even contacted Sarah, I had mentioned the basic premise to my two pals in book publishing, agent Phil and editor Chung.

Interesting idea, Phil said, but no one is going to buy it without knowing how it turns out. You must have a 'feel-good' ending.

How good must it feel? I said. What fitting, slightly fictionalized or even wholly fabricated resolution would you recommend?

And so, with all eyes on a possible producing credit, my friends came up with several tried-if-not-exactly-true, neatly-tied-up, focus-group-friendly conclusions:

- *She leaves her husband for you . . . and you both live*
  happily ever after . . .

That's good, I said. I suppose at one point it was even in the realm of eventual possibility. But (I'm just spitballing here, so bear with me): What about her family? How happy would that sort of ending play for them? Or long-suffering men—like my pals Gerry and you [Chung]—who'd instinctively identify with the husband and kids? Wouldn't they justifiably despise me for so cavalierly breaking up a marriage?

- *Point taken. Okay, slight shift in POV. The progress of*
  your emotional arc makes you available to find a newer,
  fresher love. After taking your romantic leave of Sarah,
  you immediately meet cute [movie-speak for hooking up
  in a quirky, unusual way] with a beautiful young

woman and, after a brief courtship, the two of you live
happily ever after. We can even tack on an epilogue, One
Year Later, *in which you and your beautiful young wife*
are pushing a stroller past a bookstore with your best-
selling book displayed in the window . . .

Oooh, yeah, I *like* that. I suppose it could happen. I'm just
wondering—again, just playing devil's advocate here—if we
could get away with such liberties in a nonfiction work. In
movies, I know, facts are irrelevant. But a literary audience—
especially journalistic purists—will kill us if we misstate such
gaping particulars, such as that I'm married with a child . . .
and a best seller. (What are *those* odds?)

Shouldn't we at least adhere to the salient facts? If we're
going to banner it as a true story, shouldn't the story be essentially, like, true?

- *Complete truth in advertising? Beautiful. I wish we'd*
  thought of that. So we can run a brief disclaimer, some-
  thing like: Based on a true story or Inspired by actual
  events or any other vague variation using the words
  true, actual, or real. As such, it's not outside the realm
  of reality that you could run into someone you know
  (an ex-girlfriend, say, like Connie or Francine) and
  forge a newer, deeper relationship since you're no longer
  encumbered by your idealization of Sarah . . . and then
  you two can live happily ever after . . .

Well, that seems plausible enough. In fact, Grace and I have
been seeing each other again. And now that we've renewed, re-
juvenated, and retooled our relationship, we both seem committed to make it work. But can we say with total conviction
that our ending will be a happy one? Not yet. Not by a long

shot. Besides: Just 'cause you like spectacularly variegated sunsets doesn't mean that you must have the hero and heroine walk off into them. Sometimes you've got to go it alone, and that's good, too. (Every coda need not go out on a high note; the blues are more often apropos.)

- *No problem. True and blue? We'll go with a weepie. Break their freakin' hearts. Chicks love that. We can even have you go noble a la Casablanca. Done right, that can feel damned good to an audience.*

Been damned done to death, no?

Happy Ending

My father and I would often argue about the purpose of art. I said it should reflect reality, encompassing its many seamy, unseemly, and unpleasant sides.

"At the end of a long, hard day, I don't need anymore unpleasantness," Dad would say. "I just want to be entertained."

As a judgmental young fellow, I scoffed at the naiveté of my father's escapist philosophy.

Because you don't acknowledge the ugliness in the world, I railed, won't make it go away. Only by showing it (reality) accurately will people be motivated to change it.

What a callow, naïve boob I was, presuming to lecture a man who had witnessed the actuality of the Depression (and his own mini-depressions); who had participated in and observed the authenticity of World War II; and who had daily battled the existence of lower- (and then middle-) class adult life for three-quarters of a century renowned for its seamy, unseemly reality.

Today, as the sole breadwinner (and bread-consumer) in a nuclear family of one, I want few, if any, reminders of how difficult, depressing, or downbeat life can be . . . I don't need to voluntarily submit myself to some soulless hack's violent, gritty, harsh, tedious, unvarnished, unchecked, and interminable vision of reality. No thank you, give me an amusing, moderately thoughtful, (occasionally) poignant, and thoroughly varnished view of this world. As naïve as it may be, I'll take a (believably) happy ending wherever I can find it.

I Blinked Once (and It Was Gone)

In the end, you remember the little things, the quicksilvery, slivery moments that are lost before you know they're missing. You may even learn to accept that they're gone, and even look forward to the others that lay ahead, but you never entirely lose the longing to relive *just one* before it's all over, to recapture something or someone like it was . . .

There's a concept in amateur golf called a mulligan. Essentially, after a bad tee shot on any of the 18 holes, you can choose a do-over and take another drive. Shouldn't each of us get that opportunity . . . just once?

There are, of course, no mulligans in this life. And that awareness makes every shot we do get so crucial and, win or lose, so bittersweet.

You Oughta Know

If, as many believe, age plus time equates with wisdom, then now would be a fortuitous juncture in which to offer some generic words of counsel. So, in summation:

- A good woman/man is hard to find.
- If you fall off the horse, get right back up.
- There are plenty of fish in the sea.
- The grass seems greener on the other side, but it usually isn't.
- If someone compliments half of your face, don't ask what's wrong with the other half.
- It ain't over till it's over.
- Nothing is what it used to be.
- No man is an island (unless he burns all of his bridges).
- One of life's greatest joys is sad and beautiful music.
- Play the cards you're dealt.
- Quit while you're ahead.
- Read between the lines.
- Save the drama for your mama.
- That which does not kill you makes you stronger.
- The problems of two people don't amount to a hill of beans in this crazy world.
- There are no mulligans in life, so make every shot count.
- There is no place like home.
- There is no time like the present.

- The end isn't necessarily *the end*. It's just where you are when you run out of time.
- The end is what, and where, you choose to make it.

Only Time Will Tell

That could have—*should* have—been the end. But evidently I'm not quite ready to let go, and move on. And for that, I apologize. I'm not a big fan of those works (movies, in particular) that seem to go on forever . . . or that graft on two or three pseudo finales before the last fadeout.

In a book, of course, you can't really fool anyone. You can *feel* when it's about to close. Just take your thumb and forefinger and rub out a quick guesstimate: six, eight more pages? Twenty-two, at most.

But I digress.

Here's how this book *should* end: with a party, thrown in my honor for a birthday that shall remain nameless, at my brother's home in the suburbs.

15

The One That Got Away

The End Has Begun (Reprise)

"Uncle's here!"

"Surprise!"

"Hi, Chi-Chi."

Those may be the most cheer-inducing salutations I could imagine. (Did I mention that there's nothing better than being surprised? Did I mention that this had been a pretty good year? Did I mention that, in my next book, I'm going to try and avoid so much of this singsong repetitiveness . . . which gets irritating after, say, the first four or five times?)

Look who's here: the core Boys. Andy, Joseph, Beth, Chung, Gerry, Phil, and Robert: Jew, Black, Woman, Korean, Hispanic, Irish, Italian-Gay. (We're like the archetypical platoon from a new, politically correct war movie.)

The family: sister Meryl, brother Keith. And their spouses, Dennis and Joanne. Plus, most of the cousins and uncles (all the aunts are deceased).

The kids: Alex and Zachary, my nephews and godsons, you've met. Let me introduce you to my amazing nieces—Amanda (ten) and Andi (nine)—two of the smartest, cutest, funniest women of any age you'll ever meet. I have to be especially nice to them since they're the ones who'll be taking care of me in my dotage.

Oh, and there's dad.

Dad?

No, but it sure looks like him. It's his younger brother, my uncle Lew, who's a dead ringer for my father.

Seeing me starting to choke/tear up, my friend Phil says: "Be grateful for the ones who remain."

Yeah, yeah, I've heard it before. In fact, Phil has often told me: "You spend too much time thinking about what you've lost, as opposed to what you still have."

He's right, of course. It all comes down to perception, which belief you *choose* to embrace. But I just can't help myself from thinking: This party, half over, I miss it already.

"There's still another half to go," says Phil.

Half full or half empty?

"It's your call," he says.

It's My Party . . .

Over there, lathering on the lox and cream cheese: my Ma and her boyfriend (if you can refer to a 75-year-old man as a *boy*friend). He's a good fellow. Ma's happy, I'm happy for her.

(By the way, some of you may have noticed: I don't have a date. Grace and I finally broke up for good, and bad. Neither one of us is to blame, though each of us believes in the respective rightness of our positions. There are no heroes or villains in this tale, and when all the residual hurt and anger dissipate, there will be equal parts sadness and relief . . . on both of our parts.)

But the stink of old love is still in the air. Where? Who?

Who do you think? Right over there: Sarah. And is that Bill with her? (Or did *she* bring a date?) He seems like a nice guy. Right now, the two of them are talking to Andy and Mrs. Andy about their collective four kids.

You just never know, right? Minute to minute, day to day, you can prepare, you can anticipate, you can try to control . . . but you just never know for sure what gods or circumstances have in store for you.

Day to day? That's what they say in sports after an injury: *he/she is day to day.*

"But then, again," my Uncle Stan says, "aren't we all?"

Uncle Stan!

Now there's a helluva character—he's definitely *the* man who lives each day to the fullest—who I probably should've introduced you to sooner, considering what an important role model he's been, especially in showing how close an uncle and nephew can be. He has repeatedly said that "the best, smartest move I ever made in my life was marrying my wife, Dolly. I would not have been the man I am today without her."

> **STAN**, 76, 5′10″, 196 lbs.; brown eyes; gray (once dark-brown) hair; insurance executive; my mother's sole sibling lost his wife, Dolly, to cancer after 36 years of "completely faithful marriage," then dated 129 women—he has some sort of notebook documenting his adventures—before finding Susan, his live-in love. Certainly the loss of his spouse was the biggest catastrophe of my uncle's life, but I believe his

father has been the one that got away. Grandpa Irving (born Izak Hertan) was a tough-as-dirt, old-school (before there were schools) salesman who never thought his son would amount to anything, and was not shy about reiterating this opinion. Uncle Stan became a hugely successful businessman, no doubt striving to prove his father wrong, but the palsied, drooling old man (as I remember him) died before admitting to his son (Stan) how wrong he (Irving) was.

Several times a week—from an office, which Uncle Stan swears he'll never give up ("One way or another," he says, "I'm gonna die in the saddle: making love, playing tennis, or typing out a letter at my desk")—he mails me various pertinent notes and quotes. Lately, there's been a lot of material on dating services ("I'll pay any and all costs," he says.) He's the one, much more than either of my parents, who has been constantly bugging and nudging (*noodging*?) me about getting married, saying "the right partner could make such a huge difference for you, personally and professionally." He's the one who signed me up to participate in back-to-back bachelor auctions (where, if you recall, I met a smart, pretty, vivacious shrink-in-training named Patricia-Jane, who, though 16 years my junior, was already farther along on the mental health charts). My uncle's latest kick is a service called Hurry Date, in which like-minded singles can meet up to two dozen candidates in a series of four-minute conversations . . .

Sure, Uncle Stan, I'll give it a try, I say.

"When?"

Soon, I promise.

"How soon?"

Why is *everyone* close to me so insistently demanding and unyielding?

For the time being, my powers of concentration are converging on a conversation convening barely a whisper away: two significant others from the "y-chromosomal" side sizing up each other. I've never noticed before how alike they look.

"I've seen photographs of you, and heard many stories about you," says Beth, "but it's nice to finally meet you. I imagined you'd be bigger than life."

"I think we're about the same height," says Sarah.

Then, seeing me hovering a bit too close for comfort, Beth questions: "Hey, Hemingway, what are *you* looking at?"

Me? Uh, I was just wondering: Can I get you ladies something?

"Uh, you could get *lost*," Sarah says with a mischievous, not unkind smile.

Fine, I can tell when I'm needed elsewhere. So I say, Hey, to my bud Gerry, who appears a little more down than usual. I try to cheer him up, but the poor guy is still trying to disentangle from another disastrous uncoupling.

> **GERRY,** 38 (reprise): When he began seeing "nutty Nancy," the Boys and I warned him not to get too serious too soon (on their first date, she began speculating on whose apartment could best accommodate a permanent living arrangement). When their passion finally cooled, he realized that there was no real there there, and he straightforwardly broke up with her. She responded with: "I didn't want to tell you this, but I have cancer." Being the inveterate life saver, he agreed to renew their relationship. The extent of her lunacy did not surface for another six months, when Gerry discovered that she had wholly created the illness—even forcing herself to throw up after imaginary

"chemo" sessions—to keep him from breaking up with her. At this writing, Nancy sends vaguely threatening emails to Gerry and everyone in his life, including many of the Boys (thankfully, not me), who she imagined (correctly) "poisoned Gerry" against her.

"That's it," Gerry says. "I'm done with women. Maybe Robert can fix me up with one of *his* pals."

On cue, Robert introduces us to Kenneth, his new pal (guy? boyfriend? lover? You'll often notice how even the most enlightened heteros tread lightly in these situations, careful not to say the "wrong" thing, but we would never call a *Kenneth* anything but Ken or Kenny). The boys seem good together. Good for him. Good for them. Good for anyone that finds someone.

Guys, I say to the two guy pals, could you take Gerry, our feckless friend, in tow and make sure he has a good time today?

I turn to see another buddy, Joseph, hovering over the cold cuts—and my tiny, shrinking Ma—engrossed in dialogue. With more than idle curiosity, I wonder: What's the common ground between the huge black man and the tiny white woman? Then, more serious speculation: How did my mother get so small? (Osteoporosis, I'm told.)

I espy a cute girl over by the cole slaw. Who is *she*?

Somebody whacks the back of my head. *Ouch.* What the—!?

"Don't even *think* about it," Sarah says. "That's my daughter."

Now, that would make a helluva story (and a boffo ending) . . .

But not, alas, in this life.

Look again: a young man with my blood, 13-year-old Alex, is making his move, chatting up the attractive woman ten years his senior. And she's not brushing him off. Not yet.

That's my boy.

Poor, misguided kid. Like most teenagers, he thinks he's got everything down and screwed tight. But he has *no* freaking idea what's really in store for him for the next six, or 60, years. The *freaking* alone will make his head explode.

"Would you go back and do it again?" asks my pal Chung, sidling up with a drink.

It depends.

"On?"

Whether or not they let me keep my frequent-flyer mileage.

"Did you see the 'London Journal' in [*The New York*] *Times* the other day?" Chung asks me. "It was about this British website, Friends Reunited, which originally began as a way to track down missing classmates. Now it has something like 10 million members, many of whom use it as kind of dating service that offers instant connections to ex-lovers."

"What do you know about Friends Reunited? You're just a bunch of goofy Yanks."

Martin?! You made it.

"I wouldn't miss it for the world," he says.

After the requisite 30 seconds of awkward hugs and small talk, Chung returns to business: "You're a happily married man, Martin, what would you know about Friends Reunited?"

"The London tabloids regularly run features about marriages that have broken up over affairs initiated through Friends Reunited," Martin says. "And there was a recent documentary on Channel 5 called *The Curse of Friends Reunited.* In it was this tacky bit on one woman who took up with an old beau via the Web site and cheated on her husband at their wedding."

"And what are you doing watching such down-market trash?" Robert asks.

"I was just helping out my pal here by researching the British book-buying public. It would now seem that there are millions of potential readers clamoring for a cheeky little story about the indelible nature of first love.

"By the way, is *she* here?" Martin asks me. "Your one."

Yeah, right over there. She and Beth have become old friends. I'm sure she'll be happy to introduce you.

Off they go, to see for themselves what the fuss is about, leaving me to soak in and savor this splendid gathering of dear family and friends.

Ah, you guys . . .

"Wipe that goofy grin off your face," Robert says.

Why?

"You may be able to fool some of these other *noodnicks* with this feel-good bullshit," my gay-shrink pal, Robert, says. "But I know you, and your pathology, pretty well. Failure of nerve is what I see in your actions, not necessarily nobility. If and when you find a soul mate, real love, you should not care about the consequences; you should not care about who will be hurt, even if it's yourself. Real love is ruthless. Real love is incorrigible and unaccountable. Failure of nerve is what I see in the mirror whenever I meet someone who I think could be the new one, and I find a reason to run. (You'll see: I'll find a reason to break up with Kenneth.) The difference is that I did commit once, and you never did. Not really. Until you do, it's just a lot of sound and fury, a lot of fancy words belying true feeling. And, for you, that feeling still comes down to one word: 'fear.' But don't worry, your secret is safe with me."

Then he winks. Is he kidding, or what?

Here's a world-respected psychiatrist who committed the cardinal sin by getting involved with a patient. And then that troubled soul, the live-in love of his life, took a header off their balcony. Do such events make a man more perspicuous, perceptive, and empathetic, or do they make him more conflicted, confused, and cynical?

You make the call.

One for the Boys

The next little set-to is between me and Andy, a terrific guy in every way except one: he's a huge Yankee fan.

Bullies and Suck-ups, I say of the Pin-striped faithful, just like their Boss.

For a change, however, our argument goes beyond the current despotic regime; we're disputing the talents of two Hall of Famers who began roaming their respective centerfields in New York before we were even born.

Willie Mays beats Mickey Mantle in virtually every category, I say.

"Except slugging percentage, fielding average, and knee operations," Andy retorts.

What's your point?

"If the Mick had been healthy, Mays couldn't have carried his jock."

Well, he wasn't, and he did.

"Huh?"

Well, you know what I mean.

What we both mean is that it's tough to beat a couple of middle-aged guys who've known each other forever still shooting the same old breeze.

Before you know it, Andy has to leave. As do most of the other party-goers (some reluctantly, even tearfully) as well.

What's a birthday boy to do?

"Say, 'Goodbye, Willie,'" Andy says.

Late in the Evening

There are a few long goodbyes to go, and a few die-hards yet to leave. We're sitting around the backyard of my brother's house, the drinks still flowing, the breeze still shooting. We are:

- my old flame and new best friend, Sarah;
- her husband, and my new friend, Bill;
- another ex and one of my closest friends, Beth;
- my nephew, godson and bright little shadow, Zachary, asleep, his head resting in the crook of my underarm.
- Zachary's aunt, my sister, Meryl;
- and, right in the middle of it, loving ever word, my dear ol' diminishing (in bone only) Ma.

Could it get any better, or crazier, than this? And who could have reasonably predicted such a scene ... a year ago? A month ago? Family and friends, in constant flux, contracting and expanding all the time.

I'm trying to take it all in, still adjusting to the sight of Sarah and Bill together. Yes, I know they've long been a married couple. But for so long, Bill has been a cipher, a symbol, something to consider in the abstract. It's another thing to see him paw at an (even *the*) ex-love of your life.

"I must say," Bill says to me. "I like your taste in women. Beth, Meryl, your Ma. They're all beautiful, smart, and interesting. I'm jealous."

Sarah gives him a playful whack (*my* playful whack).

"She's still mad that I never proposed to her," Bill says.

Do tell.

"Sarah gave me an ultimatum, too," he says.

What did you do?

"Well, obviously, I caved."

Immediately?

"Pretty much," he says.

"Doesn't *someone* want to marry me of his own free will?" Sarah asks.

"No man ever gets married of his own free will," Meryl says.

"You, also?" Sarah.

"Absolutely," Meryl says. "I'd still be waiting for the ring, the house, and the kids if I left it up to my husband."

"But, Sarah, it sounds like you're genuinely annoyed at Bill," Beth says.

"It would seem so," Bill says. "She brings it up in therapy all the time."

Sticking *my* nose in their business, I say to Sarah: Maybe you should get over it, give him some slack. Whereas some men might run from such a proposal, Bill stepped up and said, Yes, I want to spend the rest of my life with you.

"My son does have a point," Ma says, "though I did think he was a fool for letting you go."

"Really?" says Sarah. "I didn't think you liked me."

"I *always* liked you," my mother says. "My husband did, too. In fact, after you left, Julie swore he'd never care so much about another 'girlfriend.' He said it was 'just too painful.'"

"Marion," says Bill, "can I ask you a personal question?"

"Anything," my mother says. "I'm fascinated that you can all talk so freely about these intimate issues. In my day, this was unheard of—for men and women."

"Did you marry your soul mate?" asks Bill.

Uh-oh. Little good can come from such a question. Perhaps this is a little payback for the laundry list of questions I got his wife to air out in public. I don't want to know this answer, so I put my hands over my ears in mock seriousness and start humming. It gets an easy laugh, but I'm dead serious. There are some things, at any age, you don't want to know. Before I can look away, though, I see Ma mouth the words, "Yes, I did," and I exhale a relieved sigh.

Beth jumps in to save me (and my sister) from any further embarrassment.

"What *is* a soul mate?" she says. (Well, that question won't save *me.*)

"I'd like to answer this one," Bill says. "I believe in the concept, though I don't think I've ever experienced it myself, nor do I think most people have." [I don't know about anyone else, but I'm detecting a little passive-aggressiveness from this supposedly self-described "very not-jealous" guy.]

Bill continues: "I do believe, however, in the possibility that the two of them"—pointing to Sarah and me—"are soul mates. My wife has said as much to me and both of her therapists. [Is that another gratuitous shot?] The real question for me—and I'm guessing Meryl as well—is what to do about it? Should I say, 'So what?' and move on, or do I actually *move on?*"

"First of all, Bill," says Meryl, "leave me out of your pissing contest with my brother."

Go, girl.

"And secondly, it's not just about *soul.* For a lasting commitment, you need a bond of heart and mind, out of which comes shared goals, values, and histories."

Whoa, Sis, don't go too far.

"Get over it, Bill," Beth says. "You love your wife, she loves you, and you have two children (and a dog) who love you both. You and Sarah have been together 25 years. Some of us have trouble after the 25th minute."

My mother, adroitly trying to advance the discussion in a different direction, asks rhetorically: "Can somebody please explain to me this obsession that men have about their past? Why can't they just get over it and move on?"

Boys of Summer

"Yeah, what is it with you guys?" says Sarah. "Why can't you let go?"

Bill? I say. Do you mind if I take this one for the team? I've given it a bit of thought, especially the last few months.

"Be my guest," he says.

Boys often find glory in their drive for domination (be it in the classroom, on a ballfield, or at a dance). That first taste of victory is so sweet that, for the rest of our lives, they (we) try to duplicate or better that experience.

"But are girls any different?" Meryl says. "Don't we have similar drives?"

Probably, but I'm speaking here strictly from direct, first-hand knowledge: Men seem to have more of a problem with moving on and letting go. Women don't seem as tied to the past, or attached to a specific experience, no matter how glorious. Maybe that's because historically you haven't been steeped in such aggressively competitive culture, like sports, from an early age. Or maybe it's just that testosterone makes for different wiring than estrogen.

"Male or female, isn't that a narcissistic drive?" Beth says. "Always reliving *your* life?"

"Especially," Ma says, "when most of the women in your life weren't around to share the experience?"

Beth, you're right. When it becomes all too-consuming, it is narcissistic. Alas, the only way to conquer, or banish, the problem is to confront it head-on and dead-on. And that means considerable introspection and self-analysis.

As to your point, Ma, you're also correct. It's a selfish, even silly, desire to relive stuff that predates some of the most important people in your present life. But, when you grow too old to dream, it's nice to have someone there who remembers what you did, and who you were. With Dad gone, I think I needed someone to remind me that I was once acrobatic *and* continent.

"So this was all about having me recall a diving catch you made when you were 21 years old?" Sarah asks.

Well, not entirely.

"You are pathetic," says Beth, not unsympathetically.

Always Something There to Remind Me

As we've discussed, I ended up contacting Sarah for many reasons, not least of which jibed with her desire to call me after her father passed: to share this great calamity in the here and now with someone who knew and understood me from way back when (and who remembered my father). I thought she could help me replace what I'd lost.

"How so?" Sarah asks.

There's this *simpatico*—call it a similar sensibility, a shared perspective or just a subtly like-minded view of life—that you share with a handful of people. But since I'd just lost the one person who embodied this special nexus, it made sense at that point to try and connect, or reconnect, with someone who could perhaps help fill that void. And it has. *You* have.

"I'm jealous," says Bill. Finally: an honest response.

You needn't be. Soul mates also come in all sorts of sizes,

shapes and colors. There is not just one for everything. There are many *ones*, respectively, for lots of specific, often different, reasons. It's not a complete, one-size-fits-all package. And the affinity is not necessarily romantic. This little guy here (still-sleeping Zachary)—we've always had that thing; we just *get* each other.

"It sounds complicated," says Meryl.

That ain't the half of it.

Rage, Rage, against the Dying of the Light*

When Dad died, I felt adrift in a sea of sorrow. A little buoy that missed its moorings. But I was also flailing wildly, angry at the gods for taking him, furious *at him* for not battling harder, for going too gently into that good night.

"That wasn't his nature," my mother says, sniffling softly. "He didn't want to make trouble for anyone . . . except, maybe, himself."

I know, I know, I say to Ma. That's when I wished he had more of your fight in him. And that's also when I began to make some peace with that other part of my soul, yours, that can often make me such a combative, annoyingly insistent, obstinately persistent fellow.

With that, my voice begins breaking. I notice that my sister is already a few sobs ahead of me, and Beth soon starts in—she lost both of her parents years ago—which in turn begets a little circle of tears (excluding only Bill, I believe).

• • •

*This is the only subhead not taken from a song title, but is a line from a poem by Dylan Thomas, *Do Not Go Gently into that Good Night.*

Here's where it gets more muddled, and maybe a little bathetic.

"Pathetic or bathetic?" Bill asks.

Both. It's pathetic to observe a middle-aged man who refuses to settle for anything—or anyone—less than his heart's desire. But it's absurdly bathetic for any man or woman who believes he or she can do anything to forestall dying.

For guys (and, yes, gals) like me, reliving our past triumphs, our glory days, is a way of warding off death. It's why most athletes hang around too long. It's not the money. It's not the fame. It's the notion of immortality, your identification with or involvement in some perfect moment that lives in the public consciousness, and the possibility that (the gods willing) there could be a chance to, before you finally hang it up, duplicate it.

The inimitable Willie Mays was often cited as one of the great ones who tarnished his greatness by hanging around way beyond his prime, when his athletic skills were shot. At his retirement, he acknowledged, "It's time to say, 'Goodbye, Willie.'" It was way past time. (It probably cost him three or four points off of his career batting average and a little tarnish on his reputation.) But you had to hand it to him for *trying* to beat the unbeatable.

In the end, it's hopeless, of course. The only hope you can find is in refusing to say, Goodbye. Rage till your last breath.

"But 'goodbye' is not farewell," Sarah says. "It's just goodbye . . . for now. There's a whole other life after an athlete retires . . . or when youth comes to a close."

I know that, I say. Or I'm learning to accept that. It's all part of growing up, even if it's late in coming. For some of us (for a million different reasons), it's especially difficult to separate our idealistic youth from our pragmatic middle and old age. Even when we accept the constructs of depreciation, deterioration, and even death, it's an ongoing struggle to make peace with them.

"It's somewhat Sisyphean," Bill says.

Say what?

"The ancient myth of Sisyphus," says Bill. "The guy who pushed the rock up the hill every day, only to have it roll right down again. Sisyphus found a measure of peace—not to mention strength, honor, and nobility—when he accepted the hopelessness of his struggle."

Yeah, that's pretty good.

"What could be more poignant, or even nobly pathetic," Bill says, "than finding hope in hopelessness?"

Ain't that just another name for the blues?

Been Down So Long It Looks Like up to Me*

I am a blues man, plain and simple. I don't play them, but I do so love those same few chords and themes played over and over—they're among the saddest, most deceptively complicated and, ultimately, joyful licks in the entire musical canon. And accompanying these baleful melodies are equally resonant, moving and contradictory lyrics: *Train left the station, it had two lights on behind . . . the blue light was my baby and the red light was my mind* (Robert Johnson). *You don't want me, baby, got to*

• • •

*This is the title, not of a blues song, but of an underrated novel written by an underrated musician, Richard Farina, who died at age 29 in a motorcycle accident following an autograph party celebrating the publication of his only full-length book (after his death, a book of short pieces, *Long Time Coming and a Long Time Gone*, was published). The Doors later recorded a song called *Been Down So Long*, apparently as homage to the relatively unsung talent (who collaborated most famously with his young wife, Mimi, sister of folkie legend, Joan Baez).

have me anyhow (Mississippi John Hurt). *Got my mojo workin',
but it just won't work with you* (Muddy Waters).

"Have you ever tried to write a song?" Beth asks.

I got as far as one line: *Move on, but don't let go.*

"I don't get it," says Meryl.

"Accept your fate, yet keep on fighting," Ma says. "Right?"

Uh, yes, exactly.

"Aren't they mutually exclusive concepts?" Sarah asks.

Literally, they probably are. But the blues aren't literal, nor
do they mutually exclude. To truly know the blues, to be a man
(or a *Mannish Boy*), you're obliged hold two opposing
thoughts at the same time.

I sing: *Move on, but* don't *let go-o-o! Move on, but don't let
go. Don't let me go. Baby, don't let me go. Move, move, move, you
gotta move on, but don't ever, ever, ever let go.*

"Catchy," says Bill, "but a might repetitive."

"I think that's the point," my mother says.

Who knew? Ma *gets* the blues.

"Chi-Chi?"

Hey, look who's awake.

"Chi-Chi, don't go. Can't you stay?" Zachary says.

I'll be sleeping over tonight, Buddy. I'm not going anywhere
for a while.

"But we are," says Bill.

"Yeah, it's time," say Sarah.

It Ain't over (till It's Over)

With my six-year-old nephew clinging to my leg, I slowly walk Sarah and Bill to the door.

"Let us know how the book ends," says Bill, before heading to the men's room.

"What book, Chi-Chi?" says a small voice emanating from my ankle.

I'll tell you later.

"Chi-Chi?"

Yes, Zachary.

"What book?"

Another merciless inquisitor. It's about a werewolf and a little boy who looks a lot like you, I say, figuring that might scare off any further inquiry.

"You mean a wolfman," he says.

Later, I say, *you little monster!* (Then I tickle him into submission.)

Sarah leans in close and whispers to me: "I want to tell you something, but if you repeat it, I'll just deny it: You likely saved my marriage. Your questions and your search for answers forced both Bill and me to confront issues that were long buried. Airing them has been painful, but productive. I want to thank you for having the courage to come to me, and then to let me go. No matter what anybody else says, it was a gesture worthy of a real romantic hero."

I don't think the hero is supposed to cry, however.

"It's been great having you back in my life for the past year," Sarah continues, "and I can't imagine ever moving on again."

She pauses when we come to a black-and-white photograph framed in the hallway: a picture of my mother and father right before they got married, both looking impossibly young and handsome. (Despite the age differences, I still bear more than a passing resemblance to the man who would become my dad, and Sarah retains that dark, sultry, and foreboding look of my pre-mom). Sarah turns and smiles, a private moment between two people who'll always be a bit more than friends.

Bill arrives to take Sarah's hand; he shakes mine.

"Thanks for a memorable time," he says. "G'night."

Thank *you*, and good night.

"Speak to you tomorrow," Sarah says, lightly kissing my cheek goodbye.

Always, I say.

Stairway to Heaven

There she goes, and here I am. So much for tidy conclusions: Love walks out the door, and Grace is nowhere to be found. Not exactly what I had in mind for the perfect ending. But, on balance, probably as good as it could reasonably get.

"Chi-Chi?" (There's that disembodied voice again.)

Keith! I call out to my brother. There's a creature stuck to my leg.

"Chi-Chi! I'm not a creature. I'm your nephew."

"What's up?" Keith says.

Could you help pry this thing off me. It's on really tight.

"Chi-Chi, I'm not a thing. It's me, Zachary!"

Oh, it's *you*. How'd you get down there?

"I've been with you all day, Chi-Chi. Don't you remember?"

Sure, I do, pal, I'm just kidding.

"It's late, Zachary," my brother says, "time to go to bed. Your uncle will tuck you in."

I swing him onto my back, his hands clasped around my neck, and I carry him upstairs.

You're getting too big for this, I tell him. Soon you're gonna have to walk on your own.

"But not yet, right?"

No, not quite yet.

"Chi-Chi?"

What?

"Remember when I was almost five, and you took me to Coney Island? And we went on the bumper cars?"

Sure.

"That was fun. I wish we could do that again. Can we go back there?"

Sure.

"When?"

Soon, I tell the pint-sized sentimentalist. (Barely six, he's already pining for the good old days.)

"Chi-Chi?"

I plop the unremitting interrogator on the bed, throw him his pj's.

What, Zach?

"Tell me a story."

Excuse me.

"Tell me a story."

Uh, excuse me?

"*Please* tell me a story."

Sure. Which one?

"How 'bout the wolfman and the little boy?"

Okay.

"Chi-Chi?"

Yo.

"Don't make it too scary."

Gotcha.

"And Chi-Chi?"

Yep.

"It should have a happy ending," he says.

What would that be exactly? I ask him.

"After lots of adventures—but, remember, not too scary—the wolfman becomes a regular guy again. He moves into a house that's big enough for his nephews and nieces to stay whenever they're off from school. It has a basketball court in the driveway, lots of toys in the garage, and a freezer in the basement just for ice cream."

Is that it?

"Oh, and the house is built really, really high, just in case Bahbee wants to visit from heaven."

Is that it?

"Yes."

I can live with that.

About the Author

This talented writer's work has appeared under the byline LEE R. SCHREIBER in publications such as *GQ, The New York Times,* the *New York Observer, Fortune Small Business, Men's Fitness,* and *TV Guide.* He is the author of nine previous books, including *False Glory* (Longmeadow, 1991), a cautionary tale about steroid use in pro football (*Time* magazine cited Mr. Schreiber as "a brilliant rookie biographer") and the recent *Poker as Life* (Hearst Books, 2005). His original contribution was included among the country's top baseball writers in *Going, Going, Gone . . . The History, Lore, and Mystique of the Home Run* (HarperCollins, 2000). Now, with *The One That Got Away* (Volt, 2005), Lee Robert Schreiber has applied all of his style, humor, heart, creativity, life experiences, and, for only the second time, his entire given nomenclature to produce his most fully realized—poignant, intimate, and very funny—work of non-fiction.